THE RAINMAKER'S
TOOLKIT

THE RAINMAKER'S
TOOLKIT

*Power Strategies for
Finding, Keeping, and Growing
Profitable Clients*

HARRY MILLS

American Management Association

New York * Atlanta * Brussels * Chicago * Mexico City
San Francisco * Shanghai * Tokyo * Toronto * Washington, D. C.

This publication is designed to provide accurate and authoritative information in regard to the subject matter covered. It is sold with the understanding that the publisher is not engaged in rendering legal, accounting, or other professional service. If legal advice or other expert assistance is required, the services of a competent professional person should be sought.

Library of Congress Cataloging-in-Publication Data

Mills, Harry.
The rainmaker's toolkit : power strategies for finding, keeping, and growing profitable clients / Harry Mills.
p. cm.
Includes bibliographical references and index.
ISBN-10: 0-8144-7216-8
ISBN-13: 978-0-8144-7216-3
   1. Professions. Marketing.   I. Title.

   HF5415.55.M55 2004
   658.8—dc21   2003010062

Printing number

10   9   8   7   6   5   4

Life is like a dogsled team.
If you ain't the lead dog,
The scenery never changes.

Lewis Grizzard

Dedicated to my loving daughters Alicia and Amy.

ACKNOWLEDGMENTS

As the following list shows I have been extraordinarily fortunate to be able to call on a remarkably long list of talented colleagues, friends, clients and experts to help shape this book.

Warren Allen

Chris Aynsley

Chris Beer

John Bishop

Pat Blades

Larry Bodine

David Butler

Rob Cameron

John Clark

Kathryn Dalziel

Alaister Davis

Frank Earl

Alan Gin

Alan Good

Jim Greenway

John Hackett

Philip Hines

Peter Kerr

Roger Kerr

Terry Kirk

Jaclyn Kostner

John Link

Jim McElwain

Jeff Olson

David Parmenter

Harvey Rees Thomas

Jim Sherwin

Graeme Sinclair

Richard Stewart

Mary Tapp

Bruce Taylor

Dr David Teece

Gaynor Thomas

Richard Udovenya

Joe Vegar

Lesley Walker

John Waller

Brian Walshe

Sally Weller

Thank you all. Your feedback has invariably been practical, insightful and focused.

Michele Taylor, my personal assistant, has been a backbone of creative and tireless support.

How can you say thank you enough to a loving partner and wife who has supported you through the writing of 24 books. To Mary-Anne, all I can say is "I love you."

CONTENTS

LIST OF EXHIBITS

Chapter 4: Reacquisition

Chapter 5: Referrals

Chapter 6: Regeneration

Chapter 7: Rainmaking

Chapter 8: Related sales

Chapter 9: Reputation building

Chapter 10: Countdown to success

Appendix 1: Exploiting the Internet

INTRODUCTION

IMPROVE THE ODDS OF SUCCESS

Only a tiny minority of professional firms can consistently grow their fees and profits year in year out. While everyone enjoys patches of prosperity, few can sustain excellence for five or more years.

The goal of *The Rainmaker's Toolkit* is to give professionals the tools, techniques, and strategies they need to tilt the odds of success in their favor by helping them dramatically increase the probability of success.

HOW TO WIN CLIENTS, BOOST SALES, AND MULTIPLY PROFITS

The Rainmaker's Toolkit provides professionals with a step-by-step, easy-to-follow road map on how to build a high-profit practice founded on the principles of customer relationship marketing.

A COMPLETE MARKETING SYSTEM

The Rainmaker's Toolkit helps you to:
- Identify and turn your high-profit customers into life-long relationships
- Target high value prospects
- Close more sales—more quickly
- Increase your bid to win presentation ratio
- Build a million dollar referral network
- Master the techniques top rainmakers use to sell their expertise
- Uncover the secrets of up-selling and cross-selling
- Conduct pitches and seminars that really do produce business
- Overcome fee resistance
- Position yourself and your practice as a provider of premium services.

What Makes *The Rainmaker's Toolkit* So Effective?

- *The Rainmaker's Toolkit* dramatically increases your odds of sustainable profitable growth. The system, tools, and guidelines tilt the odds of success in your favor.

- *The Rainmaker's Toolkit* takes you further and is quicker than any other professional service marketing system. *The Rainmaker's Toolkit* includes all of the breakthrough ideas, concepts, and technologies that have revolutionized relationship marketing in the last decade.

- *The Rainmaker's Toolkit* sets out the process of building and growing your practice into logical easy-to-follow steps. A super busy professional with a full client load can manage the program.

- *The Rainmaker's Toolkit* shows you how to maximize practice profits. Here are the insights, techniques, and tools you need to create premium services for which you can charge premium fees. We show you how to stand out from the crowd by differentiating yourself from similar practices.

- You don't have to work harder to earn more. We show how to market smarter—and have fun—by doing what you enjoy.

Who Should Purchase *The Rainmaker's Toolkit*?

- Partners looking for a proven low-cost, high-return, client-centered marketing system.

- Anyone who makes marketing decisions in a professional services firm in the fields of:
  - Accountancy
  - Law
  - Consulting
  - IT and technology
  - Engineering
  - Veterinary practice

- Medicine
- Architecture
- Public relations
- Dentistry
- Outplacement and Recruitment
- Merchant banking
- Advertising
- Optometry

- Small and medium-sized professional service firms looking for a smart, low-cost way to compete with their industry giants.

- Niche, practice leaders in large professional firms looking for low-cost easy-to-implement tools to further boost revenues and profits.

- Partners in professional service firms without a specialized marketing staff who want to create a results-driven marketing culture.

- Rainmakers looking for the latest insights, thinking, and techniques on how to target and close high-profit prospects.

PART ONE

THE MARKETING CHALLENGE

CHAPTER 1

PROFITS UNDER SIEGE

*Growing your practice in
tough times*

**DOG-EAT-DOG
MARKETPLACE**

The huge $900 billion dollar professional services marketplace has become a dog-eat-dog battleground, where you need more than a big bark. The winners—the hugely profitable few—are getting richer while the rest—the vast majority of firms—struggle to maintain margins and growth. As a result, double-digit profitable growth for most professional service firms has become a distant dream.

Even practices such as the elite law firms once seen as immune to market forces are finding the going tough. A *McKinsey Quarterly* analysis of the world's largest law firms warns, "all but the most profitable are in peril."[1]

The Virtuous Cycle of Growth

The high-profit winners are growing their practices around a distinctive value proposition that will sustain high profits and double-digit revenue growth.

These high-profit, high-revenue growth firms are locked in a virtuous cycle in which they can cherry-pick top talent from their less profitable competitors and invest in expansion, new services, and cutting edge technologies.

The Vicious Cycle of Decline

The low-profit, low growth stragglers are stuck in a vicious downward spiral, losing talent and prestige at an accelerating pace until they shrink, get acquired, or simply become bit "commodity players."

Day 29 Is Here

The drive toward commoditization and price contraction continues to accelerate. A child's riddle, "The Lily Pad," captures the essence of the challenge.

> On day one, a large lake contains just one tiny lily pad.
> But every day the number of lily pads doubles, until on
> the thirtieth day the lake is completely clogged with lilies.
> On what day was the lake half full?

The answer, as bright children love to exclaim, is day twenty-nine. It takes twenty-nine days for the first half of the lake to fill with lily pads. But it takes just twenty-four extra hours for the rest of the lake to become submerged in vegetation.

Day twenty-nine is here. Three giant lily pads in the form of globalization, deregulation, and technological change are choking the professional services pond.

LILY ONE: GLOBALIZATION

Globalization has caused the creation of huge global professional service firms that can service clients across the planet. To meet client demand and stay ahead of competitors, professional service firms have merged and consolidated at breakneck pace. More than 50 percent of the world's accounting services are now provided by the top ten firms. In HR Consulting, the top ten firms control 80 percent of the total market. In IT Consulting, the top ten players share is 45 percent. In Management Consulting, the top ten control 35 percent.

Only the legal profession, where the top ten firms control less than 5 percent of the total world market, has largely been able to resist the pull. Even so, worldwide practices such as Linklaters & Alliance have formed consortiums based around a global network of offices.

At the same time, mergers and acquisition activity has exploded. Between 1985 and 1990, there were 1,140 professional service firm M&A deals in the United States worth $27 billion. Between 1995 and 2000, the number rocketed to 7,638 worth $471 billion.

The evidence is compelling. Firms in every professional service sector have aggressively invested in size and geographic coverage. A few representative examples: In 1975, strategy consultants McKinsey & Co had twenty-four offices. Today McKinsey has eighty-two offices in forty-four countries. Accounting giant PwC, formed from a merger of Pricewaterhouse and Coopers & Lybrand in 1998, has 140,000 staff and 8,000 partners in offices criss-crossing the planet. IT services giant IBM Global Services has more than 150,000 staff serving 150 countries. Advertising and communications giant Grey Worldwide has offices in 159 cities in 90 countries. Executive search firm Korn Ferry has more than 70 offices across North America, Europe, Asia Pacific, and Latin America.

Global giants such as these have the financial muscle, talent, and global stretch to compete aggressively in any market they enter.

LILY TWO: DEREGULATION

Deregulation, the second lily, has further increased competitive intensity. The Big Four accounting firms are the best example of the forces of deregulation in action. Even though they have been forced to shed their huge consultancy practices, collectively the "Big Four" still employ more than 400,000 staff. Together they still employ more lawyers than the four largest specialist legal firms combined. They still compete directly with the merchant banks for M&A work, and they still challenge HR consultants for their most lucrative consulting work.

LILY THREE: TECHNOLOGICAL CHANGE

Technological change is the third lily engulfing the lake. Accountants, for example, have watched bargain-priced software such as QuickBooks and TurboTax damage margins for certain types of routine accounting work. Clients no longer need an expensive law firm to conduct basic research when they have access to sophisticated electronic legal databases such as Lexis-Nexis and Westlaw. Who needs to talk to a fee-charging recruitment consultant when you can skim a low cost collection of online CVs?

While the Web hasn't caused the terminal damage to relationship-based services that some pundits predicted at the peak of the dot-com boom, the Internet has spawned a new generation of firms, such as E-Law.com, which provide commoditized professional services. Online recruiting has become a billion dollar industry. Online recruiting now accounts for nearly 40 percent of recruiting giant TMP Worldwide's U.S. revenue. Even the Big Four accounting firms will deliver cut-price fixed tax advice via the Web for answers to routine questions.

The firms that have flourished in this new hypercompetitive world have made marketing a central focus. They live and breathe Peter Drucker's precept: "Because its purpose is to create a customer, the business has two—and only two—basic functions: marketing and innovation. Marketing and innovation produce results; all the rest are 'costs.'"

By contrast, the underachieving laggards suffer from what I call "Marketing Deficiency Syndrome" (MDS).

Marketing Deficiency Syndrome is a "disease" that can afflict any lethargic, sclerotic, professional service firm. MDS is usually contracted by leadfooted firms that fail to inoculate themselves against market-driven changes caused by globalization, deregulation, and technological change.

The Symptoms of MDS

The symptoms of MDS appear whenever profits and growth rates stagnate and decline.

Firms suffering from MDS typically:
- Compete primarily on price, selling undifferentiated, commoditized services
- Remain heavily dependent for their survival on the continued loyalty of a few key clients
- Have a dangerously high percentage of their clients who are at risk of defection
- Lack a defined strategy for their high value clients and highly growable clients
- Hold onto their unprofitable and toxic clients far too long
- Suffer from serious deficiencies in rainmaking talent
- Lack a distinctive brand persona
- Use an inadequate and misleading set of marketing measures to track performance.

SYMPTOM 1: FIRMS COMPETE PRIMARILY ON PRICE, SELLING UNDIFFERENTIATED SERVICES

The "surplus society" has a surplus of *similar* companies, employing *similar* people, with *similar* educational backgrounds, working in *similar* jobs, coming up with *similar* ideas, producing *similar* things, with *similar* prices and *similar* quality.

Jonas Ridderstrale and Kjell Nordstrom
Funky Business

To compete in this world, the challenge is to differentiate or die, or, as Tom Peters says, "be distinct or become extinct." Yet the vast majority of professional service firms still, for the most part, sell undifferentiated services, in a form that can be bought from dozens of neighboring or competing firms.

There are essentially only two ways to compete for business. You can compete on price or you can differentiate on value and command a price premium. It is really that simple. In professional services, differentiation is the only long-term viable strategy. The reason is simple. Staff are a professional firm's main costs. Slash your staff costs, and you place your quality and reputation in serious jeopardy.

Firms who differentiate their services in ways that really matter to clients can be highly profitable regardless of their size. Look at the *American Lawyer*'s list of "Second Hundred Firms." Conventional wisdom says these firms are too small to compete with their much larger counterparts that populate the list of the "First One Hundred" law firms. Yet seven Second Hundred firms are among the United States' fifty most profitable law firms. What distinguishes these firms? "Each one is known for a dominant practice area" in which it clearly excels, be it litigation, media law, or intellectual property, reports Jim Schroeder in the *American Lawyer*.[2]

Firms such as these who differentiate on expertise charge premium fees for premium work and prosper. Sadly, most firms who suffer from MDS continue to practice SOS or Same Old Service marketing.

The Pricing Test

The number of partners in professional service firms who kid themselves they have a distinctive advantage over their competitors is amazing.

The acid test for differentiation is, are your clients prepared to pay a price premium for what you sell. If they are, they are recognizing your ability to differentiate yourself in a way that delivers value to them. Look at the House of Pricing model below.

The House of Pricing model is a simple way of looking at the way you price.[3]

EXHIBIT 1.1

The House of Pricing model

| Rooftop |
| Brand Pricing |

| Second Floor |
| Value Pricing (Exclusive Benefits) |
| **First Floor** |
| Competitor Driven |
| **Basement Pricing** |
| Cost Plus |

Basement Pricing is the lowest price you can charge and still stay in business. In essence, this is a cost plus pricing. You work out a price you need to cover your costs and add a minimum amount of profit to stay in business.

First-Floor Pricing is competitor driven pricing. You primarily base your prices on what your competitors charge. This is what most professional service firms do.

Second-Floor Pricing is value pricing. You charge a price premium because you have the ability to offer exclusive benefits, which your competitors can't match.

Rooftop Pricing is brand pricing. This is the additional premium that comes from having a brand that communicates superiority, peace of mind, prestige, and other intangible benefits for which clients are prepared to pay extra.

We estimate less than 5 percent of professional service firms have the ability to rooftop or brand price. Some fifteen percent of firms value price and reside on the second floor. The vast majority of firms, some 70 percent, use competitor-driven pricing and live on the first floor. The rest, approximately 10 percent, live in the basement, surviving on the returns from cost plus pricing.

The challenge for most firms suffering from Marketing Deficiency Syndrome is how to move from competitor-driven pricing to value pricing.

SYMPTOM 2: FIRMS REMAIN HEAVILY DEPENDENT FOR THEIR SURVIVAL ON THE CONTINUED LOYALTY OF A FEW KEY CLIENTS

The prosperity of the vast majority of professional firms hinges on the continued loyalty of a small proportion of clients. The Pareto principle—the 80/20 rule—dominates most professional services client pyramids. Year after year the top 20 percent of clients generate 80 percent of the revenues. Sometimes the figure varies slightly. The figure may be 90/10 or 75/25, but in every case a small proportion of clients delivers the great bulk of practice revenues.

Dissect the client pyramid further, and it's not uncommon to find:

- The top 1 percent of clients generate up to 25 percent of practice revenues
- The top 5 percent of clients generate 50 percent of revenues.

Exhibit 1.2 below is an example taken from one of our engineering clients. A mere 5 percent of their clients is responsible for more than half of the firm's income.

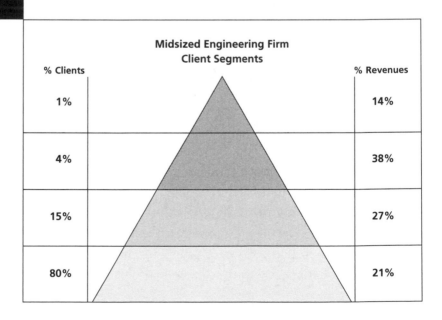

EXHIBIT 1.2

5 percent of the clients generate 52 percent of the fees

Midsized Engineering Firm
Client Segments

% Clients	% Revenues
1%	14%
4%	38%
15%	27%
80%	21%

To make matters worse, the top 20 percent of clients in most firms suffering from MDS usually generate over 100 percent of practice profits. In other words, the top 20 percent of clients commonly subsidize the other 80 percent.

Measure the profitability of the top 20 percent of clients and you'll often find that they typically earn more than 100 percent of practice profits. Look at the figures in Exhibit 1.3 taken from a large accountancy firm's business unit. The top 20 percent of clients earn 116 percent of the business units profits.

The top 20 percent of clients subsidize the bottom 80 percent

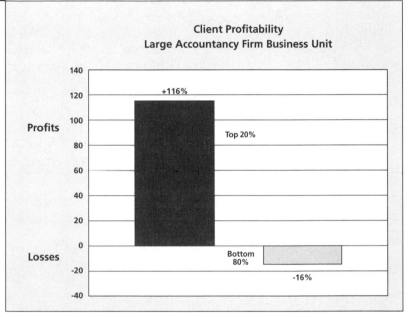

Mills Research

When the profit for each client is accurately measured and allocated, it is not uncommon for professional firms to suffer losses on 80 percent of their clients. When firms earn the vast majority of their profits from a tiny percentage of clients, the consequences of the loss of one, two, or three important clients can be catastrophic.

SYMPTOM 3: FIRMS HAVE A DISTURBINGLY HIGH PERCENTAGE OF CLIENTS WHO ARE AT RISK OF DEFECTION

"A high defection rate makes profitable growth almost impossible to achieve," says marketing professor Peter Doyle. "It is like a leaky bucket. The bigger the hole the harder the marketing has to work to fill it and keep it full."[4]

If management can increase the retention rate of 90 percent to 95 percent, then it can enormously boost a firm's growth. Compare two firms; the first loses 10 percent of its clients annually, the second loses just 5 percent. If both firms win 10 percent new clients, the first will have no net growth; the second will grow at 5 percent per annum. Over 15 years, the first firm will be unchanged; the second firm will double its client numbers.

Chris Fritsch reports that research on U.S. law firms carried out by Earl Sasser of Harvard Business School and Merry Neitlich of Extreme Marketing found that a 5 percent improvement in client retention can improve profits by 25 to 85 percent.[5]

Most professional firms foolishly think that all they have to do to keep clients loyal is to keep them satisfied. Yet client satisfaction survey after client satisfaction survey shows that 60 to 80 percent of lost clients report they are satisfied prior to defection. A large part of the problem comes from the errors professionals make when they interpret their client satisfaction surveys.

The data from most client satisfaction surveys should be broken into three categories: dissatisfied customers, just satisfied customers, and delighted customers.

Dissatisfied customers. On a 10-point scale where 10 is delighted, dissatisfied clients score 1 to 5. Because of perceived shortfalls in service performance, this group is highly likely to switch to another firm.

Just satisfied customers will score your service 6, 7, or 8 on a 10-point scale. These scores show you have met, but not exceeded, expectations. Your service is viewed as being on a par with competitors. The clients may come back, but they are vulnerable to competitive pitches.

Delighted customers rate you 9 or 10. Because your performance has clearly exceeded their expectations, these clients are highly likely to remain loyal. Most delighted clients won't even look at an approach from a competitor.[6]

Add up all the clients in the dissatisfied and just satisfied categories, and you have a true measure of the potential at-risk clients in a practice.

In most practices this figure makes frightening reading. Research on U.S. law firms carried out by Earl Sasser and Merry Neitlich found that:

- 22 percent of all law firm clients [will] consider switching firms because of problems with their current firm.
- Typically, only 25–30 percent of a firm's clients are completely satisfied.
- 70 percent or more of the firm's clients may be open to pitches from competing firms.[7]

We like to graph the at-risk clients of a firm and compare them to the at risk figures of major competitors. Exhibit 1.4 is a graphic portrait of what we typically find.

EXHIBIT 1.4

Loyal and at-risk clients

Loyal At-Risk **Client Firm**

At-Risk Loyal **Competitor 1**

At-Risk Loyal **Competitor 2**

Client Defections

The stark fact is that few professionals appreciate how vulnerable their client base is to competitor attack. The bad news for most firms is that a remarkably high percentage of their clients are at risk. The good news is that most of their competitors suffer from the same problem.

SYMPTOM 4: FIRMS LACK A DEFINED STRATEGY FOR THEIR HIGH VALUE CLIENTS AND HIGHLY GROWABLE CLIENTS

High Value Clients (HVCs) are the crown jewels in any client pyramid. The first priority in any relationship strategy must be to hold and grow your HVC business.

Highly Growable Clients (HGCs) are your future HVCs. These are good clients who have potential to grow into great clients. Identifying, servicing, and growing your HVCs and HGCs lie at the heart of any high-profit relationship strategy.

Firms with Marketing Deficiency Syndrome usually know who their HVCs are. However, firms with MDS lack any strategic or key account development process to lock up the business and fortify it against competitive attack. Firms with MDS, however, often fail to even identify their Highly Growable Clients. HGCs don't stand up and shout, "I want to be your next HVC." They are usually someone else's HVC. And since they don't spend enormous sums on your services, you won't find out what you need to turn them into a HVC without serious effort on research and rainmaking.

The first step in creating a strategy for your high value clients is to rank your clients by value. We like to start with a four tier division based on profits similar to the one shown in Exhibit 1.5.

As soon as you segment clients by profit, insights into client buying patterns begin to surface.

- **The gold tier** (the top 1 percent) typically contains the firm's super profitable clients. Typically, these clients generate large high margin fees, are highly loyal, purchase multiple services, and aren't fee driven.

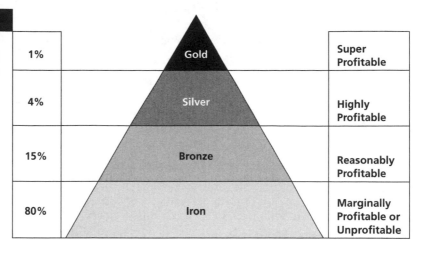

EXHIBIT 1.5

A four tier client pyramid segmented by profit

1%	Gold	Super Profitable
4%	Silver	Highly Profitable
15%	Bronze	Reasonably Profitable
80%	Iron	Marginally Profitable or Unprofitable

- **The silver tier** (the next 4 percent) contains clients that are highly profitable. Silver clients may selectively purchase only one or two of your services and often use other suppliers.

- **The bronze tier** (the next 15 percent) clients are reasonably profitable but are usually more fee sensitive, often less loyal, and may use multiple suppliers.

- **The iron tier** (the bottom 80 percent) contains the marginal or unprofitable clients. Iron clients contribute to overheads, but their low-spend or lack of loyalty means they don't deserve exceptional service.

Ranking your clients by value allows you to turn the 20/80 rule to your advantage. You can focus your service efforts on the clients who will generate the super profits and revenue you need to prosper.

You will also discover that the different segments often have remarkably different needs. We've found that gold and silver clients typically adopt a much more sophisticated attitude when purchasing professional services. Top tier clients are much more concerned about the demonstrable expertise of the service provider and by the speed of response and delivery time than the bottom 80 percent of clients. Top tier clients are much more relationship than transaction driven. Top tier clients respond positively to professionals who anticipate their needs and come up with highly customized solutions.

Top tier clients also, as a matter of course, expect service providers to have an intimate knowledge of their culture, personnel, expectations, and idiosyncrasies.

Exhibit 1.6 is a breakdown of how one of our clients, a midsized law firm, began to differentiate their clients, based on needs.

EXHIBIT 1.6

Differentiation by client needs

Midsized Law Firm	
Top 20 percent	• Relationship-driven
	• Motivated by value
	• Expect intimate understanding of needs
	• Demand access to top partners
	• Expect high-speed turn around
Bottom 80 percent	• Transaction driven
	• Motivated by price
	• Expect competent delivery
	• Value friendly service

* Source: The Mills Group Research © 2000.

From this preliminary needs analysis, the client went on to develop highly customized service offerings for their gold and silver clients (their top 5 percent).

Once you segment your client base by value and then differentiate your clients by need, you can start to exploit the full value of your current client base. Although it varies enormously from practice to practice and business unit to business unit, one in four clients have the potential to be upgraded.

It is not hard to identify gold, silver, and bronze clients with upgrade potential.

For a start, professional firms often fail to fully exploit the opportunities to sell their gold clients additional services. Silver clients can usually easily be upgraded to gold status with improved service and highly personalized offerings. The huge gains come from upgrading clients for whom you currently provide a small share of their services. These are typically bronze clients, who are some other professional firm's gold clients.

It is much more profitable to raise service levels to your top clients, rather than to raise service levels to your lower tiered clients. The reason is simple. Gold, silver, and bronze clients already trust you. They know what you can offer. All you have to do is prove you can provide extra value-added services and demonstrate your superiority to their existing provider.

By contrast, the iron clients (the bottom 80 percent) are often price and transaction driven. Iron clients often don't attach high value to the benefits an in-depth ongoing relationship can bring. They will often spurn service initiatives that will allow you to achieve a deeper, more intimate understanding of their needs.

Because of the high profitability of top tier work, a small increase in gold tier revenues will dramatically boost practice profits.

In Exhibit 1.7, a mere 5 percent increase in gold client numbers increases practice revenues by 12 percent, which leads to a 40 percent boost in practice profits.

SYMPTOM 5: FIRMS HOLD ONTO LOSS-MAKING AND "TOXIC" CLIENTS FAR TOO LONG

No business can afford to carry large numbers of loss generating clients. Yet that is what most struggling businesses do. They subsidize large numbers of such clients. The unpalatable truth is that firms often spend more time serving their loss making clients than they do courting and recognizing their high value ones.

EXHIBIT 1.7

**A 5 percent
increase in
gold clients
increases
profits
40 percent**

Whitton Strategy Consultants		
Tier One Gold Clients	**Fees**	**Profits**
81	$1,400,000	$600,000
85	$1,568,000	$840,000
Increase 5%	**Increase 12%**	**Increase 40%**

When clients do summon up the courage to get rid of their loss making clients and refocus on their HVCs, the results can be spectacular. We've watched clients double their profits within twelve months simply by eliminating half their clients and refocusing their efforts totally on their HVCs and HGCs.

Loss making clients aren't the only ones who need to be discarded. Within most client pyramids there are toxic clients. Toxic clients are those who don't pay their bills, are impossible to please, or, even worse, push you to compromise your ethical standards.

Toxic clients can cause irreparable damage. Enron's pressure on Big 5 accounting giant Arthur Andersen to legitimize its shady accounting practices caused one of the world's strongest professional service firms to disintegrate. Blue chip investment bank Goldman Sachs suffered enormous financial and reputational damage in the early 1990s by continuing to deal with British media tycoon Robert Maxwell, knowing "he was a liar and in serious financial trouble," writes Lisa Endlich in her history of Goldman Sachs.[8]

When it comes to loss making and toxic clients, it pays to heed the words of singer Kenny Rogers: "You've got to know when to hold 'em, know when to fold 'em, know when to walk away, and know when to run."

SYMPTOM 6: FIRMS SUFFER SERIOUS DEFICIENCIES IN RAINMAKING TALENT

It's virtually impossible to generate double-digit growth without superior rainmaking or sales talent. Just keeping up with normal client attrition requires a serious rainmaking commitment. Client turnover in many professional service firms fluctuates around 20 percent per year. So the ongoing sales effort for the great majority of firms has to be substantial.

"Rainmakers fish where the big fish are," says Jeffrey Fox, the author of *How to Become a Rainmaker*.[9] The difference between a good and a great rainmaker is often the size of the fish they land. Superior rainmakers catch bigger fish by focusing on lucrative clients. They know from experience that it takes just as much time to lure and land big fish as it does to land medium sized ones.

For most practices, big clients are the source of super profits. If you don't land your share of big fish, the chances are you'll go hungry or at least struggle to prosper.

"To a rainmaker, the big sale is the trophy fish on the wall," says Fox.[10]

Top rainmakers stand out for their superior sales, negotiation, and strategic account management skills.

Research shows that the top 10 percent of rainmakers sell five to seven times as much as their poorly performing colleagues who sit in the bottom 10 percent. The top 10 percent also sells twice as much business as their midrange performing colleagues. Top rainmakers are much more efficient at closing sales. They can move a prospect through the sale process much faster than their less skilled colleagues.

When it comes to face-to-face skills, top rainmakers are much more persuasive. In most professional firms, they stand out for their superior ability to:
- Establish credibility quickly
- Convert a client problem into a specific need for their firm's service

- Create urgency in a client's mind to take action
- Sell high value tailored solutions
- Anticipate and prevent objections
- Outflank competitors
- Win client commitment and close the deal.

Top rainmakers typically close a sale in 25 to 30 percent fewer meetings than their less skilled counterparts. Combine that with a low bid-to-win-proposal success ratio, and you can see why top rainmakers are so productive.

When it comes to negotiating fees and retaining margin, top rainmakers perform better. Some professionals are ineffective negotiators. They consistently leave money on the table and walk away from profitable deals.

Because they always sell the full value of the solution before they ever talk price, top rainmakers negotiate from a position of strength. They are also more skilled at win-win bargaining; trading what is cheap for them for what is valuable for their client. In simulations of fee negotiations, the top ten percent of rainmakers typically retain 25 to 40 percent more margin than that of their less skilled colleagues.

Top rainmakers are invariably superior sales strategists. A big sale involves influencing multiple decision makers and managing a complex time-consuming account management process. Top rainmakers approach their account management like grandmasters tackle a chess game—always thinking and planning three or four moves in advance.

SYMPTOM 7: FIRMS LACK A DISTINCTIVE BRAND PERSONA
In *The Invisible Touch,* bestselling author and brand expert Harry Beckwith tells the tale of "how to double your fees overnight."

> A consultant with an excellent but virtually unknown
> New York consulting firm arrived at David Schlossberg's

office in New Jersey one day, offering his services to David's firm. David was impressed with the consultant's presentation, which addressed the firm's critical need for tax consulting. David, however, was concerned about the consultant's price, which was $1,250 a day.

Within two weeks, the consultant had taken a job with a Big Six firm in New York. A week after taking the job, the consultant approached David Schlossberg again. David asked how much the consulting firm was charging. "Twenty-five hundred dollars a day," the consultant answered.

They signed an agreement that morning.

In three weeks, the consultant's market value had doubled. He had acquired no new skills and only fifteen working days of additional knowledge. He had done nothing to increase his real value; he had, however, dramatically increased both his perceived value and his price by simply acquiring a brand.[11]

Beckwith's message: "Acquire, build or align yourself with a brand." The big professional service firms treat branding seriously, because most know the value a brand makes to the bottom line. Remarkably, seven out of eight small and medium professional service firms continue to ignore branding.

SYMPTOM 8: FIRMS USE AN INADEQUATE AND MISLEADING SET OF MARKETING MEASURES TO MONITOR TRACK PERFORMANCE

Most professional firms focus on just four measures when calculating and evaluating marketing success:

- Gross fees earned
- Gross fees of the new business being acquired
- Staff utilization
- Surveys of client satisfaction.

The focus on such a limited range of measures means that client profitability, client loyalty, and competitive differentiation are virtually ignored.

As a result, practice leaders operate like the first aviators who had nothing but an airspeed indicator and a fuel gauge to tell them where they were going. In other words, the current measures provide practice managers with a rough idea where they are but about few clues where they are going. Is it any wonder so many firms lose their way?

To allocate marketing resources in a way that maximizes client profitability, and by extension firm profitability, you have to be able to also measure at a bare minimum:

- The profitability of individual clients
- The share of each client's total work or share of wallet you hold
- The lifetime value of each client
- How your firm rates in your clients' eyes when they compare you to your key competitors
- The strength of the loyalty bond that exists between your practice and your clients.

We Need a New Marketing Model

The root cause of Marketing Deficiency Syndrome is that our marketing hasn't kept pace with changes in our marketplace. The old traditional product-driven, transaction-based 4P market model (Product, Price, Promotion, Place), which has driven the thinking in many professional service firms, has always lacked relevance.

We need a new relationship-based model, one that shows professional practices how to grow, multiply, and sustain highly profitable relationships.

THE MILLS 8R MARKETING MODEL

For the last three years, the Mills Group team has been researching and field-testing a relationship-driven model and methodology that, when implemented, consistently delivers double-digit profits and growth.

The model had to pass three tests:

- Offer professionals superior insight on how to find, keep, and grow profitable clients
- Focus effort on the key marketing strategies that have the greatest impact on creating long-term, sustainable, and profitable growth
- Be memorable, easy to understand, and, above all, practitioner friendly.

The last test is much more important in professional service marketing than most professional marketers think, since much of the marketing activity in a professional service firm is carried out by working professionals for whom marketing is very much a secondary activity.

The 8R framework shows you how to maximize profits and growth by adopting a totally integrated approach to marketing. Exhibit 1.8 is a brief visual overview of the framework.

EXHIBIT 1.8

The 8Rs of client relationship marketing

R1—Revitalization: *Rejuvenate your value proposition with new services, sharper differentiation, and premium pricing.* Marketing success starts with the creation of a compelling value proposition that allows you to sharply differentiate your services from your rivals and charge the premium fees you need to prosper.

R2—Retention: *Hold onto your existing golden high-profit clients.* You'll never achieve double-digit profitable growth until you discover how to retain your high value clients longer.

R3—Reacquisition: *Win back your valuable inactive and lost clients.* Few professional firms have any formal win-back program to recapture lost clients. Yet the odds of successfully selling to a lost client are 1 in 3. Compare that to the odds of selling to a fresh prospect of 1 in 8.

R4—Referrals: *Network with the right people.* Everyone knows about referral or word-of-mouth marketing, but few know how to do it well. Referred prospects are the cheapest source of new business. It costs much less and takes much less time to close a referred prospect than a nonreferred one.

R5—Regeneration: *Target the right markets.* Client attrition means you always need to hunt for fresh prospects to regenerate and expand your client base. The key to profitable regeneration is to target and pursue profitable niches and segments where you can become the dominant player or the supplier of first choice.

R6—Rainmaking: *Close more sales while retaining margin.* With client loyalty decreasing, you need superior rainmaking and strategic account management skills to identify and win large profitable new accounts.

R7—Related Sales: *Up-sell and cross-sell to increase client share of wallet.* The odds of selling to an existing client are better than 1 in 2. So, up-selling and cross-selling to existing clients to increase your share of wallet represents a golden opportunity, which few exploit well.

R8—Reputation Building: *Brand your practice to attract premium business.* A strong professional services brand attracts and retains clients, simplifies buying decisions, and differentiates the firm from competitors. A powerful brand also adds anything from 20 percent to 300 percent to the price premium you can command.

The bottom-line benefits that come from implementing an 8R program are:
- Higher profits
- Double-digit growth
- Better clients.

BEGINNING AN 8R MARKETING PROGRAM

Before you can implement an 8R style marketing program, you need to know: which clients make up the 20 percent who deliver more than 100 percent of your profits, which clients you lose money on, and which clients have potential to be upgraded.

Start with a Client Pyramid Analysis

A client pyramid analysis segments your customers into four categories:
- Gold clients—the top 1 percent of your active clients, measured by fees or profits earned
- Silver clients—the next 4 percent of your clients
- Bronze clients—the next 15 percent of your active clients
- Iron clients—the bottom 80 percent of your active clients.

Building a client pyramid is a five-step process.

STEP 1: DRAW UP A LIST OF ALL YOUR CURRENT ACTIVE CLIENTS

Rank them top to bottom according to the fees or profits they generated in the last fiscal year. Most professional practices struggle to accurately measure profits, so it usually pays to start by ranking clients on last year's fees.

EXHIBIT 1.9 **Initial client sort based on fees**

Client Rank	Client Name	Last Year's Fees	Cumulative Fees	Cum % of Clients	Cum % of Total Fees	Pyramid Tier
1	Watson	242,000				Gold (top 1%)
2	Dawson	196,000				
3	Wilson	187,000				
40	Pine	51,000				
Ttl Gold		**3,840,000**				
41	McGill	45,000				Silver (next 4%)
200		20,900				
Ttl Silver		**3,780,000**				
201	McClean	19,000				Bronze (next 15%)
802	Jones	4350				
Ttl Bronze		**3,414,000**				
803	Garcia	1,000				Iron (bottom 80%)
4014	Ball	901				
Ttl Iron		**8,100,000**				
Grand Total		**19,134,000**				

STEP 2: DIVIDE YOUR ACTIVE CLIENTS INTO FOUR SEGMENTS:

- Gold clients—the top 1 percent of your active clients measured by fees or profits earned
- Silver clients—the next 4 percent of your active clients measured by fees or profits earned
- Bronze clients—the next 15 percent of your active clients measured by fees or profits earned
- Iron clients—the bottom 80 percent of your active clients measured by fees or profits earned.

STEP 3: SUMMARIZE THE KEY FIGURES ONTO PYRAMID CHARTS

Two examples, one segmented by profits and one segmented by fees are shown in Exhibits 1.10. and 1.11.

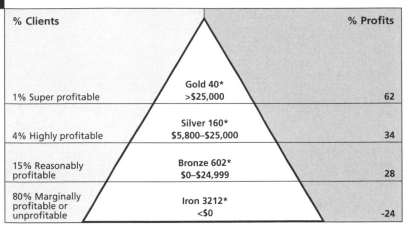

EXHIBIT 1.10

Four tier pyramid segmentation (based on profits)

% Clients		% Profits
1% Super profitable	Gold 40* >$25,000	62
4% Highly profitable	Silver 160* $5,800–$25,000	34
15% Reasonably profitable	Bronze 602* $0–$24,999	28
80% Marginally profitable or unprofitable	Iron 3212* <$0	-24

* Client numbers

STEP 4: COMPLETE YOUR PYRAMID ANALYSIS

Use a variation of the form in Exhibit 1.12 to complete your analysis. This will allow you to quickly see where you are making and losing money with your client pyramid.

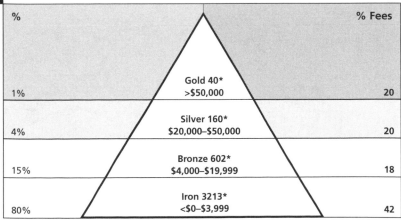

EXHIBIT 1.11

Four tier pyramid segmentation (based on fees)

%		% Fees
1%	Gold 40* >$50,000	20
4%	Silver 160* $20,000–$50,000	20
15%	Bronze 602* $4,000–$19,999	18
80%	Iron 3213* <$0–$3,999	42

* Client numbers

EXHIBIT 1.12

Pyramid tier analysis (based on sales performance)

Pyramid Tier	No. of Clients	Current Fees	Current Profits	Fees per Client	Profits per Client
Gold (Top 1%)	40	3,840,000	1,728,000	96,000	43,000
Silver (4%)	160	3,780,000	1,134,000	23,625	7,807
Bronze (15%)	602	3,414,000	756,000	5,671	1,256
Iron (80%)	3212	8,100,000	(657,000)	2,522	(204)
Totals	4,014	19,134,000	2,961,000	4,767	738

STEP 5: ADD IN TWO ADDITIONAL TIERS FOR INERTS AND LEADS

Inerts are clients, companies, or organizations that have bought services from you in the past but did not purchase any services in the last fiscal year.

Live leads are prospects, individuals, companies, or organizations whom you are currently selling to and actively trying to convert into clients.

Adding in live leads and inerts allows analysis of the size and quality of prospects that have the potential to be converted into active clients.

EXHIBIT 1.13

Six tier client pyramid (includes inerts and live leads)

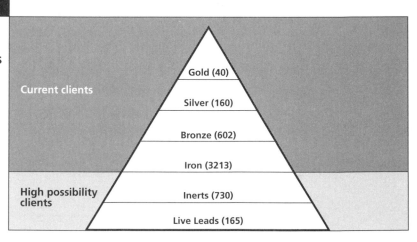

Current clients

Gold (40)

Silver (160)

Bronze (602)

Iron (3213)

High possibility clients

Inerts (730)

Live Leads (165)

Consider Using Pyramid Analysis to Set Sales Targets and Goals

Pyramid segmentation is a great tool to help you plan your sales and market campaigns. All you have to do is construct a table modeled on Exhibit 1.14. Go through your client list starting at the top. Assess each client for growth potential and set specific fee and pyramid placement goals.

In terms of pyramid placement, clients can be:
- Promoted to a higher pyramid tier
- Held or maintained at the current level, or
- Demoted or downgraded.

In particular, you are looking for the clients who have the most potential to be upgraded to become silver or gold clients.

	Current Earnings		Projected Earnings			
Client Name	Last Year's Fees	Current Pyramid Tier	Pyramid Strategy	Target Pyramid Tier	Fee Target	% Change
Morgan Ind.	$65,841	Silver	▲ Promote	Gold	$130,000	97.4
Bergin & Co.	$55,420	Silver	= Hold	Silver	$65,000	17.3
Dorlings	$53,002	Silver	▼ Demote	Bronze	$18,000	-66.0
Total	$174,263				$213,000	

INCLUDE INERTS AND QUALIFIED LEADS

Don't forget to go through your inert client list and qualified leads and set specific goals for each one also. The decisions you make here will be more speculative than the ones you make with your current active clients.

EXHIBIT 1.15

Sales targets for inactive clients*

	Historical Position			Projected Earnings		
Inactive Clients	Fees Last Year	Historical Pyramid Tier	Pyramid Strategy	Target Pyramid Tier	Fee Target
C.L. King	$21,293	Silver	Reactivate	Silver	$30,000
Allen Industries	$9,540	Bronze	Reactivate	Silver	$12,000
Frontline Software	$6,541	Bronze	Remove— not wanted	-	-

*Clients who have not provided any revenues in the last fiscal year

The real pay-off that comes from pyramid management comes when you can migrate clients from the bottom (iron) tiers into the bronze, silver, and gold tiers.

Look at Exhibit 1.16. The successful promotion of just thirty clients from the iron tier to the silver (18) and gold tiers (12) will raise fees by 8 percent and profits by 22 percent.

You can compile a table like this one to project your next year's fees and profits.

Use Pyramid Thinking to Create an Annual Client Migration

Pyramid analysis allows you to review your historical client migration patterns.
It's always useful to know how many of your clients:
- Were elevated up the client pyramid, i.e., promoted
- Stayed at their current pyramid level, i.e., held
- Dropped down the pyramid to a lower tier, i.e., demoted
- Revived from inactive to active client status, i.e., reactivated
- Became newly acquired clients, i.e., acquired
- Remained inactive, i.e., hibernated.

EXHIBIT 1.16

Promotion of thirty clients will raise profits by 22 percent

Pyramid Tier	No. of Clients	Current Fees	Current Profits	Projected No. of Clients Next Year	Projected Fees	Projected Profits
Gold	40	3,840,000	1,728,000	52 (+12)	5,002,800	2,246,400
Silver	160	3,780,000	1,134,000	178 (+18)	4,205,250	1,261,566
Bronze	602	3,414,000	756,000	602	3,414,000	756,000
Iron	3212	8,100,000	(657,000)	3,182 (-30)	8,024,340	(650,880)
Totals	4,014	19,134,000	2,961,000	4,014	20,646,390	3,613,086
$ Increase					1,512,390	652,086
% Increase					8%	22%

EXHIBIT 1.17

Last year's client migration

Movement	Number	%
Promoted	90	6.2
Held	1100	75.8
Demoted	61	4.2
Reactivated	59	4.1
Acquired	102	7.0
Hibernated	40	2.7
Total no. of clients	**1,452**	**100%**

Once you have completed a client pyramid analysis you can begin to implement the 8R marketing program. Part two of the book shows you how to implement an 8R marketing program step-by-step.

BREAKTHROUGH MARKETING SOLUTIONS

The 8Rs
of Client
Relationship
Marketing

related sales
reputation
rainmaking
regeneration
8Rs
revitalization
of client relationship marketing
referral
retention
reacquisition

TAKE THE REVITALIZATION TEST

1. Do you know the precise selection criteria your clients use to choose among competitive suppliers?

   ☐ Yes ☐ No

2. Have you compared your value proposition to your major competitors in the last twelve months?

   ☐ Yes ☐ No

3. Do you consciously plan how you can raise the public profile and reputation of your specialists?

   ☐ Yes ☐ No

4. Do you regularly assess ways to revitalize services that are under price pressure?

   ☐ Yes ☐ No

5. Have you added any new services and products to your service or product suite in the last twelve months?

   ☐ Yes ☐ No

6. Does your practice have a new service/product development strategy?

   ☐ Yes ☐ No

7. Does time-based billing (chargeable hours) still account for more than 90 percent of your revenues?

   ☐ Yes ☐ No

8. Have you reviewed the way you charge in the last twelve months?

   ☐ Yes ☐ No

CHAPTER 2

REVITALIZATION

*How to revitalize and renew
your value proposition with new
services, sharper differentiation,
and premium pricing*

Features

- Differentiating your services
- Discovering your proposition (UVP)
- Completing a SWOT analysis
- Building a client value profile
- Developing profitable new services
- Pricing for value
- Action steps

**DISTINCTION
OR EXTINCTION**

If the success formula for marketing property is location, location, location, then the success formula for successfully marketing professional services is differentiation, differentiation, differentiation.

The great sin in marketing professional services is to sell undifferentiated services. Yet the vast majority of professional firms do just that. They continue to sell me-too services. But when you sell undifferentiated services, you are simply inviting the client to buy on price.

Leadership Is the Number One Differentiator

Leadership is the most powerful way to differentiate your practice. When buyers of professional services look for success criteria to establish a benchmark, they invariably start with the market leader. Being the number one player gives you automatic credibility. Clients are much more likely to believe what you say when they know you are the market leader.

Leadership confers industry prestige. Staff from the leading firm invariably receive more invitations to deliver keynote addresses at industry conferences and get sought out by the media for expert commentaries on business issues.

Market leadership allows you to charge more. At a bare minimum, the number one player in a segment or niche can charge 20 percent more than its number two rival. McKinsey, the world's number one strategy consulting firm, consistently charges fees 25 percent higher than its closest rival.

Because buyers, especially large companies, value the peace of mind that comes from buying from the market leader, it's much easier for the number one player to grow market share quickly. Eventually, the number one player can become so dominant and influential that it can become what high-tech author Geoffrey Moore calls the "market gorilla." This leaves the number two and three market players to become the market chimps, while the remaining players compete as monkeys fighting over the remaining scraps.

The advantages of being a market leader are such that if you can't dominate the main category, you should choose a segment or niche where you can be the leader. For example, a law firm might be the second or third player in its local intellectual property market. But in the subcategory of copyright law the same firm might be legitimately able to credibly claim the number one spot. This is where the firm should consider positioning itself.

The Harvard Graduate School of Business Administration is clearly the market leader in management. So when you think of the Harvard Business School, you think management.

Wharton, the business graduate school of the University of Pennsylvania, isn't foolish enough to compete directly with

Harvard; instead, it differentiates itself from Harvard by calling itself the leader in finance.

Kellogg, the business graduate school of Northwestern University, doesn't compete head to head with Harvard. It positions itself as the leader in marketing.

Leadership Positionings

Leadership comes in multiple forms. Here is a list of possible leadership positionings:

- Market share leader   *the biggest*
- Quality leader   *the most reliable products/services*
- Service leader   *the most responsive, e.g., handling problems*
- Technology leader   *the pathfinder/first to break new ground*
- Innovation leader   *the most creative*
- Flexibility leader   *the most adaptable*
- Relationship leader   *the most committed*
- Prestige leader   *the most exclusive*
- Knowledge leader   *the best functional/technical expertise*
- Global leader   *the best positioned for world markets*
- Bargain leader   *the lowest price*
- Value leader   *the best price utility.*[1]

McKINSEY MAGIC

When it comes to positioning yourself as a market leader, no one has done it, or does it better, than McKinsey. For more than fifty years, McKinsey has been the world's pre-eminent strategy consulting firm. With annual revenues in 2001 of $3.4 billion and eighty-two offices in forty-four countries, McKinsey's tentacles stretch into and across boardrooms and governments on every continent.

McKinsey's market leadership owes much to the vision and relentless drive of Marvin Bower, who led and shaped the firm from the mid 1930s until his retirement in 1992.

Back in the 1940s, the management consulting industry consisted largely of battle-hardened veterans touting their experience and skills to corporate America. Since most businesses had dozens of seasoned troops of their own, Bower couldn't see what real competitive advantage these wizened consultants had to offer corporate clients.

Bower believed that intellect was more important than experience in solving complex business problems, so he set about recruiting the best brains from Harvard and the other elite business schools. The Baker Scholars, Harvard's top 5 percent, were targeted, courted, and snapped up in droves.

Bower particularly admired the Harvard Business School's case study approach to business problems, because it forced students to think on their feet while being interrogated by their professors. Bower thought Harvard was the ideal boot camp for McKinsey consultants who would later be judged by their clients for their ability to "foot it" and dazzle their clients with their verbal agility.

McKinsey built on this skills platform by giving its recruits intensive presentation and one-on-one interpersonal skills training. McKinsey made presentations and proposals a visible point of difference. With McKinsey you expect, and usually get, a stellar presentation.

A professional firm is judged by the quality of its clients. Under Bower, McKinsey targeted large prestigious corporates such as IBM, AT&T, and American Express. At the same time, McKinsey abandoned less glamorous clients.

Bower shifted the focus of McKinsey's work onto high level strategic issues, at the same time dropping "low level" time-management, and job evaluation studies.

This high level strategic focus allowed McKinsey to pinpoint the corporate executive suite. In the 1950s, Bower adopted a "top management approach." This meant that McKinsey would not work for a client unless it had the support of the firm's chief executive officer. Competitors said this restriction would cost McKinsey work. But Bower understood real influence and power moves from the top down.

Today, McKinsey's access to, and influence with, top CEOs is unrivaled. First-name links with CEOs are reinforced by the extraordinary number of former McKinsey staff who have become CEOs of major corporations. Today, when McKinsey recruits staff, it further differentiates itself by promoting itself as a breeding ground for future leaders. The business press reinforces this image by referring to McKinsey as "the leadership factory."

Bower didn't believe a professional firm should be seen peddling its services. So McKinsey shunned advertising. To spread the gospel, McKinsey staff published books on management, and articles in the *Harvard Business Review* and invited clients to dinner lectures and seminars presented by McKinsey staff. In 1964, McKinsey launched the *McKinsey Quarterly*, which now rivals the *Harvard Business Review* in influence. A few years ago McKinsey established The Global Institute to give it a credible voice on world economics, further extending its reputation.

The McKinsey leadership strategy has been stunningly successful. McKinsey remains the largest of the global strategy firms. It dominates its strategy consulting market with 40.6 percent (2001) market share, twice that of its nearest competitor, Booz Allen. It continues to charge huge fee premiums over its rivals, while more than 80 percent of the firm's clients are repeat buyers.

Market Specialization Is a Proven Winner

When clients choose between competing professional firms they often differentiate on expertise. A firm of specialists packed with experts commands much higher fees and is far less vulnerable to price competition than a firm of generalists. When clients consult a generalist—a general practitioner—in virtually any field, they expect and do pay much less for advice than when they seek advice from a specialist.

Positioning guru Jack Trout has for years argued that a specialist practice is much easier to market because you can focus on core service, one core set of benefits, and one core message.

Specialization, however, demands sacrifice. You have to be prepared to say no to work outside your specialty. Medical specialists do this best; you don't see cardiologists taking on hip replacements during a market slump.

WACHTELL, LIPTON, ROSEN & KATZ

Nevertheless, the rewards that come from differentiation by specialization normally outweigh the sacrifices of size. America's most consistently profitable law firm is Wachtell, Lipton, Rosen & Katz. Founded in 1965, with just one office in New York and 173 lawyers, M&A specialists Wachtell, Lipton, Rosen & Katz, earned $3,165,000 in profits per partner in 2001. The revenue take per lawyer was a staggering $1,890,000. While Wachtell ranks number one in profitability, it ranks just 47 in gross revenue on the AmLaw 100.

It's hard to find a professional firm of any type who better understands the power of specialization. Here is how Wachtell positions and differentiates itself on its Web site:

> Wachtell, Lipton, Rosen & Katz provides a unique service to our clients and enjoys a global reputation as one of the most prominent business law firms. We specialize in matters that require special attention, extensive experience, high expertise and the reputation of our partners.

> We are privileged to be involved in a very high percentage of the largest and most sophisticated merger and acquisition transactions, and also to routinely be called on to assist clients in their most sensitive and critical matters,

including "bet the company" litigation and government investigations and proceedings. We bring a focus and intensity to our work that is unparalleled.

We operate with a ratio of partners to associates of one to one, and matters undertaken by this firm are afforded the direct personal attention of partners having expertise and sophistication with respect to the issues.[2]

Here is a professional service firm that lives and breathes differentiation. New York University Professor of Marketing, Bill Starbuck's research on Wachtell reveals:

Wachtell's extraordinary success derives from its individuality. Not only does [it] differ in important ways from all organizations, it differs in important ways from the mass of law firms and. . . from other highly successful law firms. Wachtell is quite distinctive, and other law firms have not imitated its distinctive properties. . .

Wachtell's success with M&A cases arose partly from its ability to innovate, partly from its uses of teamwork, partly from its willingness to practice law 168 hours a week, partly from its self-confidence, and partly from the personalities and abilities of its founders.[3]

Recognition and reward as a specialist takes time—and follows a similar pattern across most professions. We've summarized in Exhibit 2.1 what is necessary to take advantage of the rewards that flow from specialization. Exhibit 2.2 shows how you can turn the expertise model of Exhibit 2.1 into a practical tool.

Specialization is a highly successful business model. The real profits from specialization come when you can repeatedly sell the same solution over and over again. Typical profit margins then increase from the 20 percent you can achieve on an initial project to the 70 or 80 percent you can get from delivering a variation of an earlier solution.

EXHIBIT 2.1   The rewards of specialization

	Generalist	Specialist	Expert	Authority
Stereotype	"Jack of all trades"	"Fresh faced consultant"	"Grey haired sage"	"Thought leader"
Experience/ Qualifications	Basic qualifications plus years of experience create value for client.	Typically starts with specialist postgraduate qualification. Usually requires 3 to 7 years to master tools, disciplines, and competencies.	After 10 years has solid track record in handling large, complex, high risk, challenging projects.	Honors and awards by professional peers for contribution to thought leadership or profession.
Typical Work	Relatively small, routine tasks. Refer large complex tasks to specialists or experts.	Challenging work comes with proof of increased competency. Initially builds reputation on 2nd and 3rd tier clients.	Usually works with industry leading clients.	Able to pick and choose work. Sought out for "high risk, can't afford to fail" projects.
Promotion	Downplays slack of specialist knowledge by promoting practice and experience through newsletters, brochures, and networking.	Initially builds reputation within profession by serving on specialist committees of professional association. Writes articles for trade journals. Run seminars for clients on narrow, "safe" technical topics.	Runs profession sponsored seminars for generalists within profession. Becomes "expert" news commentator on industry related issues. Delivers keynote addresses to national industry forums. Writes major articles and white papers.	Authors seminal books. Invited to speak at international conferences. Can become celebrity in own right.
Relative Income	1.0x	1.5x	3–4x	5x plus

Innovative Thinking Can Be Sold

Innovative thinking can be a compelling differentiator. Few present, package, and promote innovative ideas better than the Boston Consulting Group (BCG). Before the 1960s, McKinsey

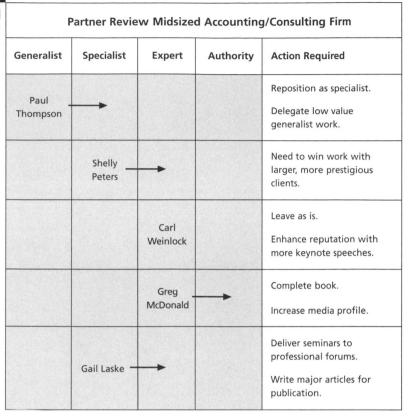

EXHIBIT 2.2

Positioning and packaging your expertise

	Partner Review Midsized Accounting/Consulting Firm				
Generalist	Specialist	Expert	Authority	Action Required
Paul Thompson →				Reposition as specialist. Delegate low value generalist work.
	Shelly Peters →			Need to win work with larger, more prestigious clients.
		Carl Weinlock		Leave as is. Enhance reputation with more keynote speeches.
		Greg McDonald →		Complete book. Increase media profile.
	Gail Laske →			Deliver seminars to professional forums. Write major articles for publication.

dominated the corporate consulting market with its ideas on how companies should be organized. However, BCG's founder, Bruce Henderson, believed McKinsey's focus produced inward looking companies. He believed corporate success came from an external focus and having the right strategy in place.

Under Henderson, BCG turned theories on business strategy into practical, easy-to-use business tools. The tool that made BCG famous was the *Product Portfolio Matrix*—or "cash cow diagram," as it is sometimes called. Henderson solved the problem of how conglomerates manage a mix of unrelated companies with an elegantly simple four-quadrant matrix (Exhibit 2.3).

Businesses in the lower left quadrant are called "cash cows." These are slow growing businesses that generate lots of cash. Companies

EXHIBIT 2.3

The Boston matrix

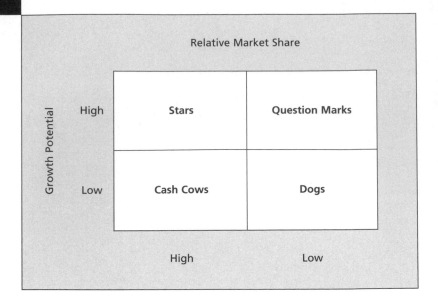

in the lower right quadrant are called "dogs." These are low growth firms that consume cash. Companies in the upper right quadrant are called "question marks." There are firms in fast growing markets that have yet to achieve their market potential. The companies in the upper left quadrant are the "stars." These are the high growth businesses that generate most of the cash they need.

Managers loved the visual simplicity of memorable labels. At a glance, managers could see how to manage their complex business portfolio. The formula was simple: milk your cash cows and use their surplus cash to feed your question marks and transform them into stars. Dogs should be abandoned or sold off.

CEOs lapped up the idea. The business press lauded BCG's insightful thinking. Business schools began teaching the matrix. Words such as "cash cow" and "dog" became part of everyday business talk. By the 1980s, the "cash cow matrix" was the most popular portfolio tool used in U.S. firms.

Henderson was so successful at packaging and selling innovative ideas, he encouraged dozens of sharply focused consulting firms to form and try to emulate BCG's success.

Being First Gives You an Edge

Starting first in a market with an idea or service is a proven differentiator. McKinsey virtually invented the field of modern management consulting. It is still perceived to be number one. Harvard was the first business school and still represents the market's gold standard.

Being first to market allows you to set the standards and position yourself in the most lucrative market segments. Being first allows you to exploit the publicity value that comes from introducing something new. Most people remember that it was Roger Bannister who ran the first sub four-minute mile. But who was the second runner to crack the barrier? No one remembers that.

In 1993, Michael Hammer and James Champy launched a whole new field of business consulting called "reengineering" with the publication of their book *Reengineering the Corporation*.

Reengineering the Corporation sold nearly two million copies. *Fortune* magazine called reengineering, "the hot new management tool," and the business press hailed it as the cure-all for what was then ailing business.

The book's publicity helped Champy's consulting firm, CSC Index, more than double its revenues to more than twice the revenues in the year following its release.

Reengineering turned into the hottest consulting fad of the 1990s. By 1994, eight out of ten *Fortune* 500 companies were reengineering their business processes, and the reengineering market had exploded into an estimated $5 billion to $6 billion consulting fees market.

CSC Index's pioneering work placed it in the perfect position to exploit this "made in heaven" market opportunity. But foolishly, it squandered its "first mover" advantage.

CSC Index made no credible attempt to protect its intellectual property. Instead it made it remarkably easy for bigger, better resourced competitors to rework and repackage its ideas by running public workshops on its methodology. Anderson Consulting (now Accenture), in particular, exploited the golden profits that were to be made in reengineering and hired thousands of extra consultants to exploit the opportunity, leaving CSC Index far behind. It didn't help that Michael Hammer and James Champy went down different paths, writing separate follow-up books advocating different approaches to solving the problems created by reengineering.

If the CSC Index story is a lesson on how to squander away the initial advantage that comes from being first, then, the Stern Stewart story is a case study on how to exploit the rewards of being a pioneer.

Stern Stewart & Co. is a global consulting firm that specializes in the measurement and creation of shareholder wealth. Stern Stewart pioneered the development of tools based on modern financial theory.

Cleverly, it labeled and trademarked its approach, calling it "EVA" (Economic Value Added). It aggressively pursued legal action against copycat companies. More importantly, it continued to add sizzle to its initial ideas by developing EVA tracking and valuation software and the preparation of EVA databases.

Stern Stewart's MVA (Market Value Added) performance rankings of publicly owned companies are now published by leading business magazines in nearly all of the major economies. Stern Stewart also publishes, in conjunction with BankAmerica, the highly respected *Journal of Applied Corporate Finance*. This magazine, plus the regular publication of books that update and revitalize EVA, means that whenever prospects think of EVA, they still think Stern Stewart.

Become a Guru

Until the early 1980s, few professionals achieved celebrity status apart from a few high profile lawyers who had earned fame through the notoriety of the clients they defended.

Then in 1982, Tom Peters coauthored the best selling book *In Search of Excellence* with a fellow McKinsey consultant, Robert Waterman. *In Search of Excellence* represented a new breed of business book. It was packaged for mass appeal with its racy anecdotes, snappy writing, and vivid examples and sold a phenomenal five million copies.

Now a star in his own right, Peters left McKinsey. His evangelical speaking style made him a hit on the speaking circuit, and soon he was pumping out a succession of additional books, as well as tapes, videos, courses, and seminars.

Peters had become a "guru," a label given to an increasingly large band of celebrity professionals who use their self-promotional skills, evangelical fervor, and message packaging talents to brand themselves as "stars."

Gurus can quickly become millionaires. Apart from Tom Peters, think of Michael Porter, Peter Drucker, Gary Hamel, and Charles Handy. All command huge consulting fees in the range of $10,000 a day. Speaking fees typically vary from $15,000 to $50,000.

The press love to quote gurus because they add character, flesh, and personality to discussions of dry, abstract ideas. Traditional academics love attacking the intellectual superficiality of much guru thinking, calling it "business pornography" and "intellectual wall paper." But the fact is, a significant portion of the business market likes its ideas cut up into easy to digest, chewable chunks.

Having a guru at the head or part of a professional firm adds considerable prestige as well as income. The guru status of Harvard's Michael Porter, for example, has been an important factor behind the rapid growth of his associated consulting group,

The Monitor Group, which in 2001 earned an estimated $300 million in fees.

Books Set You Apart

For a professional, there is no more powerful credibility builder and personal differentiator than a book. Having a book commercially published puts a halo on the author's résumé that will last the length of the author's working life. Books also add enormously to a firm's reputation.

McKinsey has long understood the power of books to sell thought leadership and expertise. Since 1980, McKinsey staff have authored more than sixty books. Some of those books have become classics of management thinking adding further mystique to the brand.

Favorable publicity from James Champy's book *Reengineering the Corporation*, saw his firm, CSC Index, grow its annual revenues in one year from $70 million to $160 million.

A successful book can turn you into a celebrity and launch a high profit speaking career. Getting a book on the *New York Times* bestseller list typically allows the author to charge $15,000 to $25,000 a day as a celebrity speaker.

In 1995, *Business Week* caught two consultants, Fred Wiersema and Michael Treacy, actively trying to manipulate the *New York Times* bestseller list by getting their consultancy firm's employees to purchase some 10,000 copies of their book *The Discipline of Market Leaders* in small quantities at bookshops thoroughout the United States. The fact that their firm was willing to spend $250,000 funding the buy-up gives an idea of the consulting income they expected to flow from authoring a bestseller.

Books are such valuable credibility builders that it's not uncommon for a busy professional to pay skilled host writers more than $100,000 to transform their ideas into readable prose.

Books provide marvelous marketing and promotional vehicles. When Alan Levins, an employment law specialist at Littler Mendelson, co-authored *The Boss's Survival Guide,* the firm's client relations department developed supporting collateral material for all of Littler Mendelson's 380 attorneys. Littler Mendelson's name and logo appear on the book's cover, and the firm created a client seminar based on the book. Littler's promotional efforts, combined with the publishers' efforts, turned *The Boss's Survival Guide* into a bestseller benefiting both parties.

Differentiate the Way You Deliver Your Service

When you join a professional firm, you quickly learn that most of your colleagues follow the same and seemingly tried and proven way of delivering their services. But there is nothing inherently superior in the conventional way most professionals or professions deliver their services. The conventional way is simply the "way we've always done it."

When forward thinking professional service firms put the conventional way of delivering under the microscope, they often discover new and different ways of creating extra value for their clients.

In his book *High Impact Consulting,* Robert Schaffer compares the conventional way most consultants work with a fundamentally different way of consulting, which he calls "high impact consulting." Compare Schaffer's high impact model with the conventional consulting model in Exhibit 2.4. Notice how Schaffer exposes the inherent weakness in the conventional model and in its place offers a highly credible alternative—one that has considerable market appeal.

Schaffer has used his high impact consulting model to differentiate his Connecticut-based firm, Robert H. Schaffer & Associates, from his competitors and in the process has created a highly successful consulting firm, servicing a galaxy of notable clients.

EXHIBIT 2.4

Conventional consulting versus high impact consulting

Conventional Consulting	High Impact Consulting
1. Defining the project	
Project goals are defined in terms of the solutions, systems, recommendations, or techniques to be provided by the consultant.	Projects are defined in terms of measurable improvements in clients' bottom-line results.
2. Determining the project's scope	
The project's scope is determined by the systems or technical issues to be studied.	The project's scope is determined by assessing what the client will be willing and able to absorb and implement.
3. Designing the project	
Projects are large-scale, with long cycle times and the speed and maneuverability of a glacier.	Projects are divided into steps to produce rapid results and to gain the experience that enables further progress.
4. Working on the project	
First the client passes the problem to the consultant; then the consultant does the job and passes the results back to the client.	The client and consultant work together as partners at every stage of the project.
5. Deploying consultants	
Large consulting teams do the work, with little client involvement.	Consultants provide focused support to client teams, who take major responsibility for the project.
Consequences	
Big up-front investments and long cycle times before value can be assessed; high risk and frequently low returns; may be little or no client learning.	Low risk, high returns; consultant time highly leveraged; short cycle time, so there is little investment before seeing a payoff; client capabilities expand with each cycle.

Robert H. Schaffer, High Impact Consulting, John Wiley, 2002, p. 46.
This material is used by permission of John Wiley & Sons, Inc.

Win an Award

In 1988, *Business Week* launched its business school rankings. Much to everyone's surprise, Harvard ranked second. Kellogg came in first, while tiny Tuck ranked third.

Much to the M.B.A. school's surprise, the results influenced the choices of the following years applicants. Suddenly, the M.B.A. factories were forced to pay attention to the opinions of their "clients" and the decision criteria recruiters used when shopping for job candidates.

All of the professions have their own equivalent of the M.B.A. rankings. The advertising industry, for example, has the Clio Awards, the Mobius Advertising Awards, and the John Caples Awards for Direct Marketing. And recognition in these can be a powerful differentiator. Just as the award of an Oscar for a film can boost this film's sales, so too can the right award boost a firm's revenues.

Awards allow you to showcase your work and win peer and client recognition for your expertise.

When the California-based engineering consulting firm Mazzetti & Associates shows its clients it has captured a raft of awards for superior mechanical and electrical work, it provides the comfort and peace of mind top prospects look for.

When Deloitte Touche Tohmatsu was honored at the 2001 International Securitization Report Awards with three first place categories for the best securitization firm in Europe, North America and Asia Pacific, it had the industry endorsements it needed to legitimately proclaim it was the best service provider in the securitization industry.

When the New York-based law firm Skadden, Ross, Slate, Meagher and Flom was ranked as the "Firm of 2001 for the Americas" by *Global Counsel 3000* magazine and selected by *Chambers Global: The World's Leading Lawyers 2001–2002* as the "USA's Business

Law Firm of the Year," it had the third party endorsements it needed to credibly position itself as a "leader among law firms."

High Price Is a Differentiator

Price influences client perceptions of quality. If you price high, clients assume you deliver quality. Many clients still believe they get what they pay for. Since buyers of professional services often have a few objective ways of comparing good from great service, high price is often the critical determinant in defining excellence.

Paying a high price can actually improve satisfaction, since it confirms we have received the best that money can buy. We expect professionals who charge high fees to know what they are talking about. In addition, we are much more likely to discount or ignore the advice of a low cost provider.

Most professional service firms price somewhere in the middle. They say, "we are not the dearest, but neither are we the cheapest." But what they are also communicating is, "we are not the best, but neither are we the worst." What persuasive value proposition does this send to the client?

The message is that if you want to differentiate yourself as a provider of premium services, you should charge premium prices.

Offer a Guarantee

The 1989 recession hit the Chicago legal community hard, particularly damaging the stellar reputation of Ungaretti & Harris, one of Chicago's leading mid-sized firms. Five years later, the firm sought to revitalize its tarnished image, needing a bold strategy to regain its quality reputation.

To get the legal and business communities focused on the firm's service and innovation, the firm Ross Fishman Marketing developed the first written service guarantee. No law firm had ever offered this type of guarantee before.

Market research showed that given the choice between qualified law firms, if one firm offered a written service guarantee, more than half would choose the firm with the guarantee.

As a result of a marketing campaign which included targeted advertising, the creation of a wide range of supporting brochures and collaterals plus aggressive media relations, Ungaretti & Harris became one of the nation's ten fastest-growing law firms.

In just *one year* (1995), during a stagnant legal market, and following five years: revenues jumped 50%, compared to the profession's 2% average growth, client retention increased significantly, more than 20 positive feature articles were written about the firm, from the *New York Times* and business press, to *The American Lawyer* and the *ABA Journal*, success in new-business competitions increased from 15% to 50%, generating millions of dollars in extra business.

The firm became known nationally as "the firm with the guarantee." Here it is:

THE GUARANTEE —

WE GUARANTEE THAT AS A CLIENT OF UNGARETTI & HARRIS YOU WILL RECEIVE COST-EFFECTIVE LEGAL SERVICES DELIVERED IN A TIMELY MANNER. WE PROMISE TO INVOLVE YOU AND COMMUNICATE WITH YOU REGULARLY. WE CANNOT GUARANTEE OUTCOMES; WE DO GUARANTEE YOU SATISFACTION WITH OUR SERVICE. IF UNGARETTI & HARRIS DOES NOT PERFORM TO YOUR SATISFACTION, INFORM US PROMPTLY. WE WILL RESOLVE THE ISSUE TO YOUR SATISFACTION, EVEN IF IT MEANS REDUCING YOUR LEGAL FEES.

Note, the guarantee is *not* a crude money-back guarantee. It is a fully fledged service guarantee.

Lots of professional service firms shy away from offering guarantees because of the perceived risk. But the fact is, most of these risks can be contained. A guarantee eliminates one of the main obstacles to buying and makes it easier for the client to say yes, rather than say no.

Differentiate the Experience

In their book, *The Experience Economy,* Joseph Pine and James Gilmore show how successful companies create experiences that tie customers emotionally to their products or services, allowing them to charge a premium.

Starbucks is the classic example. It has converted a commodity, coffee, which costs just 18 cents a cup into a $2.25 branded experience.

Pine and Gilmore use the story of the evolution of the birthday party to illustrate what they call the "progression of economic value." When our mothers (grandmothers) used to bake a birthday cake at home, mixing and baking the raw *commodities* of cocoa, sugar and flour, the cost was a few cents. When Betty Crocker and other packaged suppliers turned the ingredients into *packaged goods* in the 1960's and 1970's, the cost rose to one or two dollars. In the 1980's, most parents stopped baking cakes and started purchasing ready-made designer cakes. The cost: $10-20. Making birthday cakes had become a *service*.

What about families today? They outsource the entire party to companies such as Chuck E. Cheese, Club Disney and McDonalds. Birthday parties have become an *experience*. The cost is $200 plus.[4]

Great customer experiences are much more than the sum of the features and benefits of your services. Great customer experiences, says Bernd H. Schmitt, author of *Experiential Marketing,* "dazzle their senses, touch their hearts and stimulate their minds."[5]

To appreciate what drives a great customer experience, you need to understand the central importance of emotion. According to customer experience specialists Colin Shaw and John Ivens, "great customer experiences are created by consistently exceeding customers' physical and emotional expectations."[6]

To do this, you have to be able to focus on "stimulating planned emotions." Very few of the professional firms we have worked with have seriously addressed the challenge of how to stimulate "planned emotions." When they do they will discover, as Disney, Starbucks, Ritz-Carlton, and Harley Davidson have, that great customer experiences are a source of long-term, sustained competitive advantage.

In the 1980's, marketers focused on quality and service as the keys to differentiation. In the 1990's "build a brand" became the dominant talk. Don't be surprised if "build a great customer experience" becomes the catch cry of marketers in the first decade of the twenty-first century.

DISCOVERING YOUR UVP

In the 1950's, adman Roger Reeves said the key to successful advertising was to identify something in a product or service that made it unique. Reeves labeled it the USP—the *unique selling proposition*.

But professional services rarely have a single unique selling proposition. Successful differentiation in professional services comes from combining multiple features into a *unique value proposition (UVP)*.

Most services share a number of common features with their competitors. These are the *points of parity,* the core features you must offer to be a legitimate, credible provider.

The features that differentiate your services and set you apart are the *points of difference.* Market success comes when you discover the potent combination of points of parity and points of difference, which are your UVP.

Testing Your UVP

While there are multiple ways to differentiate your services, a successful UVP should meet three tests:

1. Does our unique value proposition generate client value?
2. Can we sell our UVP?
3. Is our UVP sustainable?

Generate client value. To be successful your UVP must add value. Does it reduce costs, improve performance, or raise satisfaction? In the final analysis, it doesn't matter how good you think your UVP is. The only opinion that counts is that of the clients.

Can the UVP be communicated? To be successful you have to be able to communicate and sell your UVP. With services that are often invisible and intangible, this sometimes can be a major challenge.

Is our UVP sustainable? Service differentiators can be easy to copy. The challenge is to create a UVP that is difficult to emulate.

Exhibit 2.5 is a checklist of professional service differentiators. Use it to compile your own list of differentiators.

COMPLETING A SWOT ANALYSIS

A traditional SWOT analysis, which examines the strengths and weaknesses of your practice and identifies what opportunities and threats you face in the marketplace, will often provide additional insights you need to create a sustainable competitive advantage.

A partially completed SWOT analysis is shown in Exhibit 2.6. You can complete a SWOT analysis on several levels:
- For the practice as a whole
- For each market segment
- For each major service line
- For the competition.

EXHIBIT 2.5

Competitive
differentiators
checklist

Firm-wide Capabilities·	Points of Parity	Points of Difference
• Firm profile/reputation	☐	☐
• Technical superiority	☐	☐
• Pioneer in industry/market	☐	☐
• Strength of research and development	☐	☐
• Large base of satisfied clients	☐	☐
• List of notable clients	☐	☐
• Track record of continuous innovation	☐	☐
• Endorsement by opinion leaders	☐	☐
• High market share	☐	☐
• Superior management /leadership	☐	☐
• Depth and breadth of expertise	☐	☐
• Depth and breadth of creative talent	☐	☐
• Breadth of products/services	☐	☐
• Integrated range of services	☐	☐
• One-stop shop	☐	☐
• Size of firm	☐	☐
• Entrepreneurial/enterprising style	☐	☐
• Reputation within profession	☐	☐
• Ability to continually meet tight deadlines	☐	☐
• Financial resources	☐	☐
• Shared vision/culture	☐	☐
• Geographic coverage	☐	☐
• Location of offices	☐	☐

Knowledge and Expertise Capabilities	Points of Parity	Points of Difference
• Technical superiority	☐	☐
• Quality of work	☐	☐
• Speed of project completion	☐	☐
• Thought leadership of top partners	☐	☐
• State-of-the-art products /services	☐	☐
• Unique intellectual property	☐	☐
• Service/product innovation	☐	☐
• Technological innovation	☐	☐
• Revolutionary ideas	☐	☐
• Superior industry knowledge	☐	☐
• Superior staff qualifications	☐	☐
Relationship Capabilities		
• Intimate knowledge of client	☐	☐
• Depth of personal relationships	☐	☐
• Accessibility of partner in charge of job	☐	☐
• Adaptability and responsiveness to change	☐	☐
• Absolute trust and confidence	☐	☐
• Ease of working with staff	☐	☐
Value Adding Capabilities		
• Ability to provide competitive edge	☐	☐
• Ability to transfer knowledge	☐	☐
• Highly competitive pricing	☐	☐
• Business results focus	☐	☐
• Ability to deliver measurable results	☐	☐
• Highly accountable	☐	☐
• Results-driven pricing	☐	☐

EXHIBIT 2.6

Partially
completed
SWOT analysis

SWOT ELEMENT	ACTIONS NEEDED
Strengths	**Capitalize on Strengths**
Partner expertise	Promote through new public seminar program
	Advertise success in client industry journals
Weaknesses	**Address Weaknesses**
Inexperienced associates	Develop intensive up-skilling program
	Pay retired partner to act as mentor/coach
Opportunities	**Maximize Opportunities**
Expand risk management	Plan portfolio-related services
services	
Threats	**Minimize Threats**
Acton Associates Management	Buy out Acton and offer partnership to their
Services perceived to be	leading authority
number one in risk	
management	

BUILDING A CLIENT VALUE PROFILE

We've designed a tool called The Client Value Profile to help you understand why clients buy from you. The client value profile will help you identify the areas where you need to build new capabilities and in the process revitalize your value proposition.

Exhibit 2.7 is a completed customer value profile. The firm with the highest score has the best total value proposition.

How to Complete the Client Value Profile

1. *Market Description.* Describe the market, segment, or service line or business unit under analysis.
2. *Selection Criteria.* List all the factors that your clients will consider when choosing a supplier. If you need help selecting decision criteria, use the list of competitive differentiators (in Exhibit 2.5) as a guide.
3. *Performance Scores.* Score yourself and each of your competitors 1 to 10 (1=disastrous; 10=outstanding).

EXHIBIT 2.7

Client value profile

Market Description					
Selection Criteria	Your Score	Best Comp. Score	Comp. 1	Comp. 2	Comp. 3
technical expertise	10	9	9	8	9
industry knowledge	8	7	7	7	5
quality of work	9	8	8	8	7
competitive fees	7	8	6	6	8
firm reputation	8	9	8	9	7
depth of team	8	8	8	7	7
meeting deadlines	7	8	8	7	7
access to partner	9	8	8	7	8
range of services	8	9	9	9	8
location of offices	8	8	8	7	7
geographic coverage	8	8	7	8	7
Performance Scores 1–10 (10 = Best)					

In Exhibit 2.7, you are clearly the supplier of first choice. This is the type of value proposition that allows you to grow and prosper and in time become the number one player in your market.

DEVELOP PROFITABLE NEW SERVICES

Once you understand your market and what your clients are looking for, you should begin to develop new services. If you don't develop new services or revitalize your existing ones, you'll eventually stagnate and die.

In their study of more than 1,500 new service launches, Canadian professors Robert Cooper and Scott Edgett found new services:

- Enhance your reputation
- Increase customer loyalty
- Make cross-selling of existing services easier
- Entice new customers to use existing services.[7]

Cooper and Edgett found the top performers they studied had clearly defined innovation strategy, the resources in place to meet development needs, and a high quality development process.[8]

What Is a New Service?

A new service doesn't have to be a revolutionary breakthrough. There are few truly revolutionary service developments. A new service means a service that *from the customer's perspective* represents a change; "*new* is a change that affects or is noticeable to a client."[9]

Clients look to their professional service providers for innovative service to give them a competitive advantage. Firms who, year after year, continue to offer up the same service menu soon find themselves facing declining client loyalty, loss of client share, and shrinking margins.

The top professional service firms are always coming up with innovations that create a competitive edge for their clients. New York's premier law firm Wachtell, Lipton, Rosen & Katz developed the poison pill to deter hostile takeovers. Merchant bank Salomon Brothers developed mortgage-backed securities.

Much of the recent profitable growth in the professional service market has come from new products and services, especially in IT related areas. Much of Accenture's explosive revenue growth in recent years to its current annual revenues of more than $11 billion can be put down to the rapid development and application of innovative new practices, products, and services.

To stay in front with service innovation, practice leaders need to keep asking three key questions:

1. What existing services can we revitalize to better meet our changing client needs?
2. What extensions to our existing service lines can we develop?
3. What new services and products can we develop to improve our competitiveness?

The Service Innovation Test

To be successful, a new service must be tested against six criteria:

1. **Target market.** To be profitable an innovation requires a receptive customer base that will support and sustain it.
   Ask: What types of clients will be interested in our innovation? How might they purchase our service and how often?

2. **Need.** Clients must value and be prepared to pay for your innovation.
   Ask: What real benefit does this innovation offer our clients? What price premium will a potential client be prepared to pay to use our new service?

3. **Unique advantage.** The benefits must be seen as unique. Imitation services that provide the same benefits as competitors have little value.
   Ask: What unique advantage does innovation offer? Are there existing services that provide essentially the same benefits?

4. **Speed.** Speed to market is often important. The first mover captures much of the credit reputation and market accolades.
   Ask: Can we launch this service quickly enough to gain the first mover advantage?

5. **Sustainability.** Services that can be instantly copied have less long-term value. The innovator needs to develop barriers to entry. The most effective deterrents to competitors are usually brand building, superior marketing, and speed to market.
   Ask: What can we do to lock in and sustain our competitive advantage long term?

6. **Management commitment.** New services take time, resources, and refinement to become established and start generating sizable cash flows.
   Ask: Will top management commit the time and resources to give this innovation time to take off?

The Eight-Step New Service Development Process

New professional services are too often the result of random inspiration. To dramatically improve the odds of success, you need to follow a disciplined step-by-step new service development process.

Here is a tested eight-step development process:
1. Define the business problem
2. Research multiple solutions
3. Screen out impractical, unworkable, and obviously unprofitable ideas
4. Refine concept into a testable market proposition
5. Analyze the costs of development and potential cash flow
6. Test market your new service
7. Scale up and refine your delivery systems
8. Market and launch your new service.

STEP 1: DEFINE THE BUSINESS PROBLEM

To create high-profit service innovations, you have to deliver unique benefits that customers are prepared to pay for. The best place to start is with your customer's most intense, most frustrating, most time-consuming problems.

EXHIBIT 2.8

The eight-step new service development process

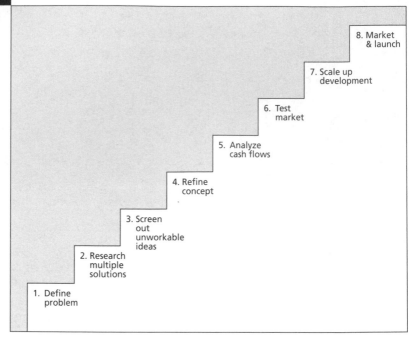

8. Market & launch

7. Scale up development

6. Test market

5. Analyze cash flows

4. Refine concept

3. Screen out unworkable ideas

2. Research multiple solutions

1. Define problem

The ideal customer problem is large, complex, and urgent. Clients will pay premium fees to solve such problems.

Use the 5 to 1 problem-to-fee ratio to assess whether the problem is large enough to justify the development of new services. The 5 to 1 problem-to-fee ratio says a client's problem should be worth approximately five times the fee you can charge to solve it. In other words, a million dollar problem would justify a $200,000 fee.

Complex problems are ideal because they require lots of expertise to solve and usually can't be solved in house. Urgent problems are ideal because they command top priority when budgets get allocated.

The number one reason new services fail is there is no need. In other words, the clients don't believe they have a problem big enough to invest money and time in solving.

To help you create high value solutions, it is very useful to categorize the problem you are trying to solve into five types.

Ask yourself, does the solution:

1. Prevent the problem?
2. Solve part of the problem?
3. Solve the problem differently?
4. Solve a related problem?
5. Solve a broader problem?

Use the problem analysis form (Exhibit 2.9) to generate creative solutions.

EXHIBIT 2.9

Problem analysis form

Problem Categories	Possible Solutions
Prevents the problem	
Solves part of the problem	
Solves the problem differently	
Solves a related problem	
Solves a broader problem	

Craig Terrill and Arthur Middlebrooks, Market Leadership Strategies for Service Companies (NTC, 2000), p. 151.

Involve your clients in your discussions as soon as possible. In spite of their best intentions, few professional service providers think or behave like their typical clients.

STEP TWO: RESEARCH MULTIPLE SOLUTIONS

Most problems can be solved or at least managed in a number of ways. So don't settle on a single approach until you've tested multiple solutions. Often the best ideas come when you are prepared to move outside the square and consider radical approaches.

STEP THREE: SCREEN OUT IMPRACTICAL, UNWORKABLE, AND OBVIOUSLY UNPROFITABLE IDEAS

Be ruthless. Successful new service innovators are ruthless. Weed out unpractical, unworkable, and, above all, unprofitable ideas.

Few firms have the resources to blindly test multiple innovations. So only test market those innovations with high upside potential.

STEP FOUR: REFINE YOUR CONCEPT INTO A TESTABLE MARKET PROPOSITION

Clients will not buy vague concepts. Clients buy specific services that solve specific problems. They need to understand how it is to be implemented and how it differs from what is already in the marketplace. The more details the better.

Prepare a full-scale visual PowerPoint style presentation on what the service is, how it works, and what benefits it delivers. Then put the presentation before a selective group of critical clients.

Keep refining until clients possess a crystal clear picture of what your service is and what benefits it brings. If the presentation doesn't generate excitement with your trial audience, go back to the drawing board.

STEP FIVE: ANALYZE THE COSTS OF DEVELOPMENT AND POTENTIAL CASH FLOW

Most services dramatically underestimate the costs of development and are over-optimistic with their cash flow forecasts. If possible, use outside consultants with a proven track record in new service innovation to critique your figures.

STEP SIX: TEST MARKET YOUR NEW SERVICE

If possible, test your new service in a market you know and understand. Be ambitious when you set your minimum targets for success. Remember that the purpose of the test market is to check whether the financial assumptions you made in step five are correct. If you fail to meet your minimum goals, abandon the project or go back to the drawing board.

STEP SEVEN: SCALE UP AND REFINE YOUR DELIVERY SYSTEMS

A high percentage of service innovations fail because of poor execution or inadequate resources. If you create a need you can't fulfill, you are simply working for the competition.

STEP EIGHT: MARKET AND LAUNCH YOUR NEW SERVICE

Invest heavily in the launch. If you don't have in-house resources, hire a PR firm to generate publicity. Involve the rest of the firm. Everyone, including the most traditional parts of your firm, benefits from service innovation.

Service innovation and the ability to charge premium fees are closely linked. Success as a service innovator requires a sound business strategy, disciplined service innovation process, a willingness to experiment, and the courage to be different.

PRICING FOR VALUE

When Accenture (formerly Andersen Consulting) broke away from Arthur Andersen in August 2000, it set a series of remarkably ambitious revenue goals. Despite the recession and tech bust that savaged other consulting firms, Accenture recorded a revenue increase of 17 percent to $11.4 billion. The rest of the industry grew at half that rate.

Part of the success is due to a change in how Accenture gets paid for its work. *Forbes* magazine reports Accenture "is moving away from the old model of hourly fees and towards a pay-for-performance. Some 80 percent of its revenue now comes from performance-based and fixed-price deals up from 50 percent five years ago."[10]

The Sacred Cow of Hourly Billing

The great enemy of value pricing is hourly billing. As professionals have come to divide their work time into *billable* and *nonbillable* hours, they forget what matters is value not hours.

Ronald Baker, the author of *The Professional's Guide to Value Pricing,* points out there are lots of pluses to hourly billing:
- Hourly billing is a relatively easy and efficient pricing method
- Hourly billing is a useful cost accounting tool
- Hourly billing transfers the risk to the client.

However, these pluses are minor when you look at the huge minuses.

Hourly billing misaligns the interests of professional and client. There is an inherit conflict of interest between the client's need for speedy work and the professional's need to clock up time.

Hourly billing focuses on hours, not value. When most professionals have to defend price they talk hours, where they should be selling value. Skilled sellers always sell the value first and talk price last.

Hourly billing punishes you for introducing timesaving technologies. Why bother to innovate if you are going to earn lower fees?

Hourly billing does not differentiate your firm. When you bill by the hour, you convert your expertise, insights, experiences into an hour—a taxable commodity—which allows you to be traded off against competitors.

Hourly billing limits your income potential. There are only so many hours you can charge in your year.

Charging for Value

If you sell value you should charge for value delivered. Exhibit 2.10 is a list of the ways professionals charge for their services. Each one has its pros and cons. But if you are determined to become super profitable, you will have to use "value billing" whenever you can. This does not mean you should not discard hourly billing altogether. Top billers mix and match their pricing methods.

Consider each one as you look for your optimal pricing solution. Don't be constrained by one model. They work best when used in combination.

Exhibit 2.11 contains fifteen questions you need to ask when you price a proposal. Consider each one before you settle on the appropriate pricing strategy. Once you have considered the questions, you can choose an optimal pricing strategy.

How to Charge Value-Based Fees

Here are the critical do's and don'ts when setting value-based fees. Determine the value before talking price. Before you can accurately set a value-based fee, you must know three things.

1. What is the client's ultimate objective? Do they want to increase sales, cut costs, or raise customer satisfaction?
2. How will the client measure progress or success? You have to know what success criteria the client will use to judge completion.
3. What is a successful result worth to the client? If you succeed, what quantifiable value will you actually deliver? You can't charge $100,000 for a solution that is only worth $70,000 to the client. On the other hand, you can easily charge $100,000 if you know the solution is worth $700,000.

Avoid premature discussions on fees. If the client prematurely asks, "how much will this cost?" answer, "I can't give you the answer until I have a full understanding of your needs. As soon as

EXHIBIT 2.10 Alternative pricing models

Pricing Model	Description	Pros	Cons
Time-based charging • Still very common in law, accountancy, and consulting	• Basically a cost plus billing system	• Simple to understand, easy to document • Overcomes tendency to underestimate completion times for projects • Relatively transparent to clients	• Focuses on efforts, not results • No direct link to value • Severely limits income potential
Tender • Common in government and where tenderer wants to ensure lowest price	• Secret competitive bidding designed to maximize competitive pressures	• Allows buyer to easily compare prices for like services	• Process implies service commoditized • Difficult to establish value
Retainer as a deposit against future services • Common when seller unsure of being paid	• Guarantees access to seller's services for agreed amount of time	• Offers greater security of income	• No direct link to value generation
Availability only retainer • Sometimes called "pure retainer" or "right to call retainer"	• Payment for nonspecific services at a future time	• Seller may not have to perform any services • Client guaranteed access	• Limits ability to work for competitors
Fixed fees • Becoming much more common in consulting and advertising and IT projects	• Total price estimated and fixed up front • Can easily be combined with hourly fee for those areas that can't be defined	• Certainty for client • Much easier to sell total value of solution	• Risk of underestimating time to complete • Not always practicable where high uncertainty
Retrospective pricing • Surprisingly common among top-billing professionals	• Professional bill at end of arrangement based on his judgment • Value added • Needs trusting relationships	• Value linked • Allows you to deliver greater than expected profit before you bill	• Client has no price certainty—professional's and client's perception of value may differ • Can increase fee disputes
Commissions • Common in advertising (% media billed) • Common in equity underwriting (% size of deal)	• Usually charged as % of total transaction	• Quality and value can be sold • Can be super profitable	• % of transaction size is crude measure subject to misuse • Perception of unearned margin • Commission rates in most industries have fallen over time

Pricing Model	Description	Pros	Cons
Membership fee • Increasingly being offered as Web-based client lock-in service	• Annual fee typically allows access to range of services, such as conferences, subscriptions, online forums	• Deepens relationship • Good way to add value	• Precise value difficult to quantify • Limited situations where it can be used
Performance improvement fee • More common in consulting projects where value can be quantified	Fee linked to: • Increase in revenues • Cost savings • Increase in profitability	• Intimately linked to value • Large potential fees for vendor • Simple for client to calculate	• Clients sometimes resent high payouts
Success fee • Common in merchant banking • Contingency fees very common in U.S. legal profession	• Variation of performance based fee • Can be combined with base fee	• Strong incentive to deliver results • Usually super profitable if you win	• Clients sometimes resent high payments • Not a good tactic if aim is intimate, long-term relationship
Licensing • Ongoing payment for access to proprietary research, tools, and software • Commonly used with training courses	• Basic annual fee with additional payments tied to ongoing use	• Value different for each client, since fees strongly linked to knowledge used	• Key ideas difficult to protect • Methodologies and ideas often easy to copy • Compliance costs and issues
Joint venture • Partnership where both parties share risks and rewards	• Clients take a % share of business in return for large long-term partnership	• Long-term total alignment of interests with clients • Clear sharing of risks and rewards	• Difficult to exit from if problems • Potential for conflict of interest
Equity and stock options • More common when stock market buoyant	• Typically cash-poor client offers equity in exchange for fees	• Very strong incentive to deliver long-term value • Potential for super profits	• Significant downside risk
Royalty • More common where knowledge can be embedded into a product such as software	• Upfront development costs usually borne by vendor • % fees based on ongoing sales or fees	• Where product or service has a long service life, returns can be huge	• Low, if any, initial fee • Compliance costs and issues

EXHIBIT 2.11

Questions to ask before setting your fee

1. How much time and labor is involved?
2. How big is the client's problem?
3. How complex is the client's problem?
4. How urgent is the problem?
5. What is the market rate for equivalent work?
6. What is the potential loss or gain for the client?
7. What demonstrable extra value can we add?
8. What is the nature and length of the client relationship?
9. What evidence is there that we are the only firm who can realistically perform this work?
10. What is the experience, reputation, and talents of the professional who will deliver the services?
11. How price-sensitive is the client?
12. Is the work for an individual, corporate, or government client?
13. How profitable or wealthy is the individual or organization?
14. What are the odds of high quality repeat work?
15. How strategically important is this work for our firm?

I do know what you require, I can be back to you with a price within 24 hours. Is that ok?"

Offer your clients multiple options. Wherever possible give your clients a range of choices including a budget option. Giving your clients a range of yeses works much better than presenting them with a single yes/no choice.

Focus on the performance improvements, not on your problem-solving ability. Virtually all professionals can solve problems. But few professionals can improve the performance of already top class operations. That is where the value is.

Quantify your benefits. Strive to achieve a minimum 5 to 1 benefit to cost ratio. The perceivable tangible and intangible improvements you create should be worth at least five times the fee to the client.

Highlight the differences between you and your competitors. Spell out what makes you distinctive. Highlight the tools, methodology, and processes that allow you to achieve breakthrough results that make you unique.

Ask, don't tell. The more involved the prospect is in the needs diagnosis, the more likely he is to buy into your recommendations. Keep asking questions until you understand the problem inside out. And when you do locate the problem, don't rush in with a solution. Sit on the problem until the client takes ownership of the problem and fully appreciates the full size and complexity of the issue.

Remember that what buyers say they want and what they actually need are usually two different things. Remember also, small, simple problems require low price, off-the-shelf solutions. Large, complex problems require sophisticated, high value solutions.

Customize your recommendations. Tailor each of your recommendations to the prospect's precise needs.

Where you can, use their exact words and phrases when you present your recommendations. Tailored recommendations minimize objections. Clients are much less likely to haggle over price if you've provided them with "exactly what they want."

Use independent third party endorsements to support your claims. Most clients are sceptical until offered proof. In professional services where quantifiable proof can be difficult to obtain, endorsements from respected third parties can be incredibly powerful.

Don't voluntarily offer discount options based on a promise of increased future work or the acquisition of multiple assignments. This tactic simply encourages the buyer to negotiate hard on price and make promises (usually false) about the future volumes of work you'll get if you slash your margins.

Practice explaining your new fee structure to clients. It's surprising how difficult most professionals find it to state "our fee is $52,500" and follow up with a value-based explanation. Most professionals need at least two hours of training and role-playing on how to state and explain a change in billing practice.

If you do have to cut your fee, negotiate the nonprice tradables. Clients often have the power to offer lots of valuable "nonmonetary" tradables. They can provide you with referrals to their clients; they can help you get to speak at their trade association conferences. It's rare to find a situation where you can't find opportunities for a mutual win-win exchange.

If the client says no to your proposal, be prepared to walk away. Don't be fearful of rejecting business that doesn't meet your requirements. Simply say to a client, "I would like to work for you, but I can't work for you on this, based on what you are offering for this assignment. I would like to keep in touch. Perhaps we can find a project that meets both of our needs."

You'll be surprised how often the buyer backs down at this point. If you do have to walk away, remember, the best deals are often the ones you walk away from.

Finally, never apologize for what you charge. Remember, all you are asking for is an equitable share of the extra value you've created.

ACTION
STEPS

1. Use the list of competitive differentiators to start to develop your unique value proposition (UVP).

2. Use the positioning and packaging of your expertise tool to plan a specialization strategy.

3. Use the critical success factor analysis tool to review your competitive strengths.

4. Assemble a "new service team." Ask them to identify:
   - What existing services can be revitalized to better meet our changing needs?
   - What extensions to our existing service lines can we develop?
   - What new services and products can we develop to improve our competitiveness?

5. Set up a formal, disciplined, step-by-step new service development process.

6. Critically review the way you currently charge for services.

7. Use the price model diagram to identify a range of possible value-based pricing strategies, which will allow you to move toward value-based billing.

8. Establish a target that *x percent* of your revenues by *y date* will come from performance-based and fixed-price deals.

9. Train your professionals on how to charge value-based fees.

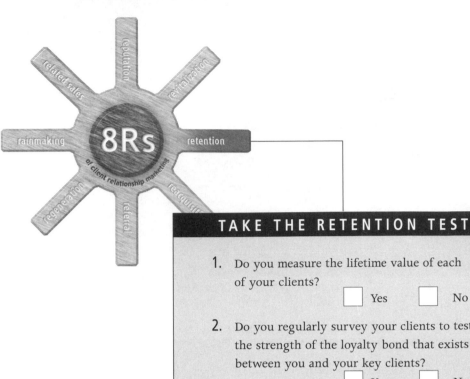

reputation · related sales · revitalization · rainmaking · **8Rs** · of client relationship marketing · retention · regeneration · referral · reacquisition

TAKE THE RETENTION TEST

1. Do you measure the lifetime value of each of your clients?

   ☐ Yes ☐ No

2. Do you regularly survey your clients to test the strength of the loyalty bond that exists between you and your key clients?

   ☐ Yes ☐ No

3. Do you know what impact a 5 percent increase in retention per annum would have on your practice profits?

   ☐ Yes ☐ No

4. Do you know what percentage of your practice profits come from loyal clients who have been with you over five years?

   ☐ Yes ☐ No

5. Do you have a high value client (HVC) marketing program specifically aimed at retaining and growing your key clients?

   ☐ Yes ☐ No

6. Do you know whether you are the supplier of first choice with your key clients?

   ☐ Yes ☐ No

7. Are your frontline staff trained and empowered to solve complaints quickly?

   ☐ Yes ☐ No

CHAPTER 3

RETENTION

*How to hold onto your
high-profit clients for life*

Features
- The economics of retention
- Retaining the right clients
- Turning satisfaction into loyalty
- Loyalty and handling
- New insights into customer service
- Defection is bad, downward migration is worse
- Action steps

THE ECONOMICS OF RETENTION

Ever since the publication of Frederick Reichfeld's book *The Loyalty Effect* in 1996, it has been an article of faith, certainly, among professional service marketers, that highly profitable clients are by definition loyal clients.

According to Reichfeld, loyal clients are more profitable because they cost less to service. New clients are more costly to serve because it takes time to learn their requirements and set up systems and processes to serve them. Loyal clients are more profitable because they are prepared to pay more for the same services. Finally, loyal clients are much less likely to haggle over prices. Reichfeld's reasoning seemed to make sense, and it was certainly what most professionals wanted to hear.

Then in the July 2002 *Harvard Business Review,* two business researchers, Werner Reinartz of Insead and V. Kumar of the University of Connecticut, published a damning critique on the notion that loyal clients are by definition highly profitable.[1]

Reinmatz and Kumar found that lots of the long-standing customers they researched (40 percent) were barely profitable. A high percentage of loyal but barely profitable clients know their value to a supplier and unashamedly exploit the length of the relationship to demand and get premium service.

Instead of always being prepared to pay more, Reinmatz and Kumar found that long-term customers often pay lower prices than new customers. Because long-term customers are often more knowledgeable about a supplier's services, they strongly resent suppliers who dare to take advantage of the length of the relationship.

Reinartz and Kumar's research doesn't mean you should forget about building client loyalty. Sixty percent of the long-term clients they analyzed were in fact highly profitable. What Reinartz and Kumar are saying is:

1. Never assume a loyal client is a profitable client.
2. Measure and analyze every customer relationship.

That way you can focus your efforts on retaining the right clients.

RETAINING THE RIGHT CLIENTS

Once you know who your profitable clients are, you can begin to work on how to hold onto them. A high defection rate of profitable clients quickly turns a goal of high growth into a fantasy. Most practices simply don't have the marketing muscle to win enough new clients to compensate for the good clients who defect.

One of the easiest and quickest ways to select clients who will have high lifetime value is to ask four questions.

1. Which clients are of strategic importance?
2. Which clients are significant revenue contributors?
3. Which clients are profitable?
4. Which clients are loyal?

EXHIBIT 3.1

Which clients are valuable?

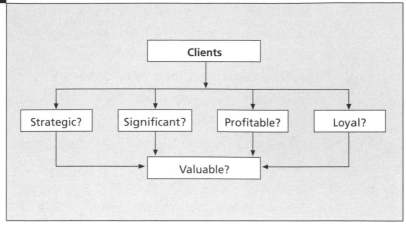

Adapted from Jeremy Hope and Tony Hope, Competing in the Third Wave *Harvard Business School Press, 1997 p. 115.*

QUESTION 1: WHICH CLIENTS ARE STRATEGICALLY IMPORTANT?

Clients are strategically important if they give you the opportunity to grow because:

- They represent an ideal customer type. They love what you offer and mesh perfectly with your core competencies.
- They have good growth prospects. They could be in a strong growth market or possess a competitive edge.
- They are highly influential. They can help you break into new markets.
- They can teach you about new technologies, markets that are critical to your long-term future.
- They provide valuable referrals to other business.

QUESTION 2: WHICH CLIENTS ARE SIGNIFICANT REVENUE CONTRIBUTORS?

A client is significant because it provides a sizeable percentage of your revenues. Typically, it might sit in the top 10 percent of your accounts.

Size always demands attention. But beware—not all large accounts are profitable. Large unprofitable clients need urgent attention. Large clients *should be* the largest contributors to profits.

Sizeable clients often represent huge untapped potential. Ask, "Do we have all their business, or are we low on their list of suppliers?"

QUESTION 3: WHICH CLIENTS ARE PROFITABLE?

Even though it is sometimes difficult to accurately measure individual client profitability, ask yourself:

- Do the clients always pay on time?
- Do they ask for extended credit?
- Do they always look for discounts?
- Do they require high working capital or staff support?
- Are they difficult to work with?

Don't just examine profitability for the current year. Much more important is the lifetime profitability of the client.

QUESTION 4: WHICH CLIENTS ARE LOYAL?

Some clients are inherently more loyal than others. When judging your clients on loyalty, you may like to use the following classifications:

- *Devoted fan:* Relationship driven and will always purchase from you
- *Regular supporter:* Routinely purchases from you but also buys competing services
- *Fickle supporter:* Blows hot and cold and is unstable and unpredictable
- *Promiscuous:* Transaction driven and is fundamentally disloyal.

Use the client evaluation profile shown in Exhibit 3.2 when you assess the potential value of your client base.

EXHIBIT 3.2

Client evaluation profile

Strategic	Significant	Profitable	Loyal	Actions
Yes	Yes	Yes	Yes	• Deliver extraordinary service • Develop unique personalized services • Create collaborative partnerships
Yes	Yes	Yes	No	• Become "trusted advisor" to key decision-makers • Identify long-term "lock-in" opportunities
Yes	Yes	No	Yes	• Repackage value proposition • Negotiate higher fees
Yes	Yes	No	No	• Cut costs • Up-sell and cross-sell
Yes	No	Yes	Yes	• Sell enhanced value proposition
Yes	No	Yes	No	• Sell new services
Yes	No	No	Yes	• Sell new value proposition
Yes	No	No	No	• Being strategic is not enough. Review
No	Yes	Yes	Yes	• Deliver exceptional service
No	Yes	Yes	No	• Delegate work or outsource wherever possible
No	Yes	No	Yes	• Size is not enough. Raise fees or exit
No	No	Yes	Yes	• Develop growth strategy
No	No	Yes	No	• Delegate or outsource work
No	No	No	Yes	• Raise prices or cut costs and service levels
No	No	No	No	• Exit

Adapted from John O Whitney, "Strategic Renewal for Business Units," Harvard Business Review, July–August 1996, p. 91; Jeremy Hope and Tony Hope, Competing in the Third Wave, Harvard Business School Press, 1997, pp. 115–120.

Further Pointers to Profitable Loyalty

Clients who start by paying the full price right from the beginning are more likely to stay loyal than clients who begin the relationship when attracted by a price promotion. Discount fees attract price-driven buyers. They will push for better prices or leave. It may seem initially more daunting to attract new clients who will pay you full fee, but it will invariably pay off in the long run.

Referrals make better prospects than those who respond to advertisements and other public promotions. Loyalty from referrals is more powerful because the referral is an extension of an existing relationship. This is why referral marketing is so powerful and why referral marketing must form a key part of any loyalty building program.

"Long courtships are better than short ones," says customer relationship expert and author Tony Cram.[2] "Like human relationships, whirlwind romances *can* turn out to be one-night stands. Those customers who take a long time to woo, and insist on getting to know you well, are more likely to stay with you for the duration."

Clients who want highly personalized offerings are more likely to become loyal. When this group receives highly tailored, individualized support, it usually responds with loyalty.

Clients with special needs often value long-term relationships. Certain clients require highly sensitive, highly discreet service. Clients such as these value the confidentiality and trust of a long-term relationship.

Clients who receive extra help at a critical phase in their history often reward their suppliers with extended loyalty. Going the extra mile and providing extra help at times when clients feel particularly vulnerable pays off in the long term.

Watch out for clients and prospects who exhibit these six traits. These are the clients who have the potential to become the "crown jewels" in your golden client pyramid.

TURNING SATISFACTION INTO LOYALTY

Most professional firms naively believe that all they have to do to keep their clients loyal is to keep them satisfied. They make the mistake of believing that satisfaction is the same as loyalty. They couldn't be more wrong. Customer satisfaction survey after customer satisfaction survey shows that between 60 percent and 80 percent of all lost customers report they are *satisfied prior to defection*.

What then is the link between satisfaction and loyalty? Most customer satisfaction surveys measure satisfaction on a 1 to 5 scale, where 5 is "very satisfied" and 1 is "very dissatisfied." Customers who place themselves at the extreme ends of the scale hold intense feelings about the company.

APOSTLES AND TERRORISTS

The very satisfied act as "apostles." They love the service, so they act as an unpaid sales force, enthusiastically recommending your service to others.

The highly dissatisfied feel just as intensely. But their negative experiences have turned them into "terrorists." They actively bad-mouth you to anyone who will listen.

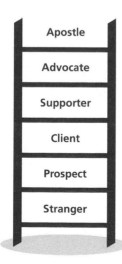

BEWARE THE ZONE OF INDIFFERENCE

The customers who reside in the middle of the satisfaction scale and rate themselves as a 2, 3, or 4 fall into a *zone of indifference*. Because they feel indifferent to you, they are prepared to be courted by other suppliers. There is therefore little relationship between their satisfaction score and loyalty.

The loyalty message is: To merely satisfy customers is not good enough. A client who scores 3 or even 4 out of 5 on a 5-point scale, where 1= low, is vulnerable to competitive attack. To make clients loyal you have to wow them. The goal of your satisfaction program must be to make all of your high-profit or potential high profit clients apostles.

HOW TO MEASURE SATISFACTION

Highly satisfied clients repurchase again and again. Xerox found its highly satisfied clients (apostles) were six times more likely to repurchase than customers who described themselves as merely satisfied.

Exhibit 3.4 is a client satisfaction survey modeled on the template. It will give you much of the base information you need to build a rock solid client loyalty program.

HOW TO MEASURE LOYALTY

When you get your client satisfaction surveys back, remember the three critical questions are the first three in the survey that ask:

- What was your "overall level of satisfaction"?
- Would you use the service again?
- Would you recommend our service to others?

Research by Burke Customer Satisfaction Associates, a leading U.S. market research firm, confirms that a client who is very likely to stay loyal is:

- Highly satisfied with your current service
- Would definitely do business with you again
- Would definitely recommend you to others.[3]

EXHIBIT 3.4

Service Being Measured

Overall level of satisfaction:

1. What was your overall level of satisfaction with our service?

   ☐ Excellent   ☐ Very good   ☐ So-so   ☐ Dissatisfied   ☐ Strongly dissatisfied

2. I would use the service again.

   ☐ Strongly agree ☐ Agree   ☐ So-so   ☐ Disagree   ☐ Strongly disagree

3. I would recommend this service to others.

   ☐ Strongly agree ☐ Agree   ☐ So-so   ☐ Disagree   ☐ Strongly disagree

E=Excellent   VG=Very Good   G=Good   F=Fair   P=Poor
5=Extremely Important 4=Important 3=Somewhat Important 2=Neutral 1=Not at All Important

Attribute/Quality Indicator	Not Observed	Performance	Importance	Comments
Delivers promised results	N/O	E VG G F P	5 4 3 2 1	
Technical expertise	N/O	E VG G F P	5 4 3 2 1	
Industry expertise	N/O	E VG G F P	5 4 3 2 1	
Easy to work with	N/O	E VG G F P	5 4 3 2 1	
Excellent client references	N/O	E VG G F P	5 4 3 2 1	
Competitive fees	N/O	E VG G F P	5 4 3 2 1	
Meets deadlines	N/O	E VG G F P	5 4 3 2 1	
Overall reputation	N/O	E VG G F P	5 4 3 2 1	
Reputation of key staff	N/O	E VG G F P	5 4 3 2 1	
Transfers expertise to clients	N/O	E VG G F P	5 4 3 2 1	
Depth of team	N/O	E VG G F P	5 4 3 2 1	
Accessibility of top partners	N/O	E VG G F P	5 4 3 2 1	
Full range of services	N/O	E VG G F P	5 4 3 2 1	
Geographic coverage	N/O	E VG G F P	5 4 3 2 1	
Location of offices	N/O	E VG G F P	5 4 3 2 1	

General Comments:

Here is what I like best about your service.

What aspects about our service or quality need improvement?

Additional comments:

So, any client who doesn't rate this highly on all of these three criteria must be treated as vulnerable.

Moments of Truth and Loyalty

Jan Carlzon of Scandinavian Airlines used the term *moment of truth* to define "any instance when a customer comes into contact with some aspect of your organization and has an opportunity to form an impression" about the quality of service you deliver.[4]

Collectively, these moments of truth define your client's experience and together create the generalization they use to describe your firm.

A simple but remarkably potent way to increase loyalty is to create "wow" experiences for your clients at each moment of truth.

Use the form in Exhibit 3.5 to identify your clients' moments of truth and wow experiences.

EXHIBIT 3.5		
Wow experiences– positive moments of truth	**Moment of Truth**	**Wow Experience**
	1.	
	2.	
	3.	
	4.	
	5.	
	6.	
	7.	
	8.	

LOYALTY AND COMPLAINT HANDLING

A sophisticated complaint handling system is central to building a highly loyal client base. Technical Assistant Research Programs (TARP) research over the last thirty years has found problems decrease customer loyalty by 15 to 30 percent.

The bad news is that for every five customers who have a problem, you risk losing some, if not all, of the future revenue from at least one of those five customers. The good news is that you can protect this income stream by preventing or fixing the problems with better service.

MOST DISSATISFIED CUSTOMERS DON'T BOTHER TO COMPLAIN

On average, TARP found 50 percent of consumers and 25 percent of business customers who experience problems can't be bothered to complain.

Customer service researchers, Shycon Associates, found that almost 70 percent of corporate purchasing agents would take immediate punitive action against a company without complaining. Companies report it is easier to switch vendors than complain.

To make matters worse, those who do complain don't use the formal complaint handling system. They usually pass on their gripes to whomever is available or willing to listen.

Customers who are dissatisfied with a company's services tell twice as many people about their bad experience as those customers who are delighted with a company's services. Add to this the fact that bad news travels three to four times as fast as good news.

TARP estimates that one potential customer will be lost for every fifty potential customers who hear a negative word of mouth.

SUCCESSFUL RESOLUTION OF COMPLAINTS INCREASES LOYALTY

When customer problems are successfully resolved to the clients' satisfaction, these clients tend to be more loyal than those who never experienced a problem in the first place.

This represents great news for practices that are prepared to set up effective complaint handling systems, especially when you consider the typical cost of resolving a complaint compared to the cost of winning a new customer.

Loyalty decreases when it takes more than one follow-up call to fix an issue. Loyalty also decreases if a company only mollifies or appeases the customer (that is, the customer is not completely satisfied, but the action is acceptable).

REAL LOYALTY COMES FROM REAL DIFFERENTIATION

Even wow levels of service will not keep your clients loyal if there are chinks in your competitive armor. Uniqueness increases retention. What makes your services unique not only makes them easier to sell; the more different (or less substitutable) your service is, the greater your retention rate. Give a client access to *identical* services and the probability of repeat business and loyalty drops markedly.

CROSS-SELLING INCREASES RETENTION

Cross-selling additional services improves retention. The more relationships a client has with your firm, the higher the retention rate and the client's lifetime value.

Managing Client Expectations

Clients do not judge a service on its own merits. They judge it relative to their expectations. This is a critical issue in professional services, since professionals play a large role in setting client expectations. When you raise client expectation beyond what you can reasonably deliver, you are setting the client up for disappointment and dejection. Client expectations have to be consciously managed so that the end result is delight rather than disappointment.

Firms need to train professionals in how to manage client expectations.

Edward Yourdon wrote a book called *Death March* as a warning to software developers who engage in "Mission Impossible" projects. The warnings should be read by all professionals.

OVERSERVICE FIRST-TIME CLIENTS

It pays to make a super effort with "first-time" clients. They are still working their way into a relationship with you and are much more susceptible to defection than second-time and other repeat clients.

According to customer loyalty expert Jill Griffin, "first-time buyer attraction is often double that of older accounts."[5]

Remember—first-time clients don't know how you work, and there is a good chance you don't fully appreciate their needs. So the chances of a misstep are relatively high.

NEW INSIGHTS INTO CUSTOMER SERVICE

Most professional service firms feel good service is simply a matter of common sense. However, some insightful new thinking has come from research in the behavioral sciences. American academics Richard B. Chase and Sriram Dasu have distilled the research from behavioral science on customer service into five new operating principles.

PRINCIPLE 1: FINISH STRONG

When it comes to managing the beginnings and ends of a service encounter, the end is of critical importance. "The end is far more important because it's what remains in the customer's recollections," say Chase and Dasu. [6]

When consulting, for example, they advise not to deliver all the golden nuggets of wisdom at the front end of the assignment. Hold back a few nuggets for the end of the engagement. If you do, the client will report much higher levels of satisfaction.

Remember, "last impressions—not first impressions—endure." Chase and Dasu advise that "even if you can't end with a substantive bang, it's smart to finish with a stylistic flourish."[7]

PRINCIPLE 2: GET THE BAD EXPERIENCES OUT OF THE WAY EARLY

In professional services bad experiences typically come packaged as bad news. Most clients want to hear bad news straight away—but most professional service providers delay passing on bad news until the last possible moment.

This is the worst thing you can do, say Chase and Dasu. "Get bad news, pain, discomfort, long waits in line, and other unpleasantries out of the way quick fire"[8] so they don't dominate the customer's recollection of the entire experience.

PRINCIPLE 3: SEGMENT THE PLEASURE, COMBINE THE PAIN

When gambling we prefer to win $10 by winning $5 twice, but when it comes to losing $10, we prefer to lose the $10 in one blow. The reason, behavioral scientists say, is that people have an asymmetrical reaction to losses and gains.

When you apply the notion to service, it means you should break pleasant experiences into lots of stages but group unpleasant experiences into one single stage.

PRINCIPLE 4: BUILD COMMITMENT THROUGH CHOICE

Would you believe it? Blood donors report they experience far less discomfort when they are allowed to choose the arm from which the blood is to be taken.

The reason is that we are much happier and more likely to be satisfied when we believe we have some control over a process, especially when the process involves discomfort. Several airlines, for example, now let passengers choose when they want to have their meal served during a long flight.

Wherever possible, give clients choices especially when it comes to choosing between two undesirable alternatives.

PRINCIPLE 5: GIVE PEOPLE RITUALS AND STICK TO THEM

Most professional firms don't appreciate how ritualistic people are and how rituals provide meaning and comfort in service encounters.

"Rituals," say Chase and Dasu, "are particularly important in longer term professional service encounters. They're used to mark key moments in the relationship, establish professional credentials, create a feeling of inclusion, flatter customers, set expectations and get feedbacks."[9] Common rituals include kick off dinners, elegant PowerPoint presentations, weekly summary calls and progress reports.

The impression a distinctive style of PowerPoint makes on clients is remarkable. Color printers allow you to create stunning handouts, yet remarkably few professional firms take advantage of the new low-cost reproduction technologies.

Small lapses in rituals can easily shift a client's impression from success to failure. Remarkably, clients will often blame these lapses later for the reason a project has gone wrong.

"More ominously," say Chase and Dasu, they can "shift a customer's perception about the quality of the service, the service providers, and the company they represent."[10]

The message is clear: ritualize your service encounters wherever possible and stick to them.

DEFECTION IS BAD, DOWNWARD MIGRATION IS WORSE

Most professional firms become so consumed in preventing client defections that they often fail to notice a larger problem, downward migration. Research by McKinsey shows many more customers change their spending behavior than defect. McKinsey calls the customers who spend less "downward migrators."[11]

A two-year study across sixteen industries in markets as different as airlines, banking, and consumer products shows the bottom line impact of downward migration is "surprisingly large."[12]

At a retail bank McKinsey studied, 5 percent of checking account customers defected annually, taking with them 10 percent of the bank's checking accounts and 3 percent of its total business.

"But every year the 35 percent of customers who reduced their balances cost the bank 24 percent of its total balances."[13]

The Causes of Downward Migration

McKinsey found that downward migrators fall into three groups.

1. *Lifestyle downward migrators.* This group spends less because its needs have changed.
2. *Deliberative downward migrators.* This group frequently reassesses its purchase decisions, always looking for the best option. When it does decide to move, it bases its decisions on rational decision criteria.
3. *Dissatisfied downward migrators.* This group comprises actively dissatisfied customers who typically have become disenchanted because of a bad service experience.

The best professional service practices already monitor downward migration—especially among their top tier clients. The best are also reasonably good at fixing the service breakdowns that cause active dissatisfaction.

Few, however, seriously or systematically address the threat posed by lifestyle migrators, that group of customers who are reassessing their loyalty because of their changing needs.

ACTION
STEPS

1. Identify clients with high potential lifetime value.

2. Set up a customer satisfaction, measurement, and management program that permeates every level of practice.

3. Set up complaint handling, tracking, and resolution systems.

4. Train all staff to provide immaculate levels of service.

5. Empower staff to use their judgment when action is required to make things right.

6. Train staff so that all who service have a good working knowledge of the products and services you deliver.

7. Train professional staff on how to set and manage client expectations.

8. Identify the "moments of truth" in your service cycle and create a list of specific "wow" enhancers to create positive memories.

9. Increase your service levels for "first-time" clients.

10. Develop a set of service strategies aimed at cementing the loyalty of your highly valuable clients (HVCs).

    • Give all who deal with HVCs the tools, knowledge, and training they need to identify, greet, and service HVCs face-to-face and on the phone.

    • Empower staff who deal with HVCs with higher levels of discretion to resolve HVC issues.

    • Develop special services that are exclusively for the use of HVCs.

    • Benchmark your services and satisfaction levels against competitors who also service your HVCs or represent potential competition.

11. Identify all of your HVCs who have significantly reduced their spending in the last fiscal year.   These are the downward migrators.

    • Identify those who have reduced their spending because of a change in their needs. Ask what you can do to address these.

    • Identify those who are reducing their spending because of changes in their buying criteria. Resell what originally made you their first choice. Then identify ways you can meet their changing priorities.

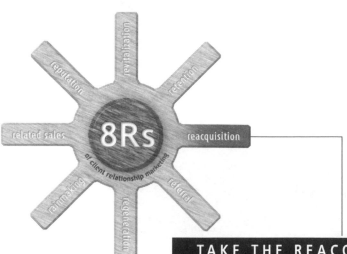

TAKE THE REACQUISITION TEST

1. Do you know how many clients you lose each year?

   ☐ Yes ☐ No

2. Do you identify such a client in your database as lost?

   ☐ Yes ☐ No

3. Does your practice monitor at-risk clients who look likely to defect?

   ☐ Yes ☐ No

4. Do you interview lost clients to analyze why they defected?

   ☐ Yes ☐ No

5. Do you know what percentage of your lost clients you actually win back?

   ☐ Yes ☐ No

6. Do you have a specific program to recapture lost clients?

   ☐ Yes ☐ No

7. Do you calculate the cumulative lifetime value of each of your clients?

   ☐ Yes ☐ No

CHAPTER 4

REACQUISITION

How to recapture your inactive and lost clients

Features
- Recapturing lost clients is highly profitable
- How to win back lost clients
- How to detect at-risk clients
- How to save at-risk clients
- Action steps

RECAPTURING LOST CLIENTS IS HIGHLY PROFITABLE

Most professional firms write off former clients as a lost cause—and transfer their energies into client acquisition. That's plain dumb, when you appreciate that client win-back is much more profitable than acquisition.

Research shows:

- The chances of successfully selling to an existing client are better than 1 in 2
- The chances of successfully selling to a lost client are 1 in 3
- The chances of successfully selling to a fresh prospect are 1 in 8.

Why is it that acquiring new clients is less profitable than recapturing lost clients? The big advantage you have with lost clients over fresh prospects is the information you have on them:

- You know how to contact them
- You know what they like and dislike
- In many cases, you know how to read their behavior
- You know the ins and outs of their firm's decision-making process.

The figures clearly show that client reacquisition should be a high priority in any client relationship marketing program.

DEFECTION BLINDNESS

In 1999, customer loyalty experts Jill Griffin and Michael W. Lowenstein surveyed 350 U.S. businesses from a cross-section of industries about their firm's customer defection and win-back practices. They found:

- Few firms are aware of their true customer defection rates
- Most companies do not have strong win-back policies, programs, or monitoring systems.

Few professional service firms we have worked with have win-back policies in place.

Griffin and Lowenstein report that every year the average U.S. firm loses 20 to 40 percent of its customers.[1]

Evidence from our own professional service client base suggests that the defection rate for most professional service is significantly lower than this. However, the rate varies enormously from professional service group to professional service group. Some professional services such as auditing encourage long-term relationships. Others, such as consulting, which is much more project based, have a much higher defection rate.

WHY DO WE SUFFER FROM DEFECTION BLINDNESS?

Why are we so ignorant when it comes to client defection and putting in place policies to recapture lost clients? There are four reasons:

1. **Most firms put all their energies into acquisition and retention.** That's not surprising when you consider that's what the vast number of books, articles, and seminars on customer loyalty have espoused in recent years. As a result, most firms fail to take, set up, and implement the programs they need to recover lost profits.

2. **Firms misinterpret their client retention rates.** Griffin and Lowenstein show "defection rates of 50 percent can masquerade an 80 percent retention rate. A defection rate problem can disguise itself in healthy retention figures." [2]

   "Assume," say Griffin and Lowenstein, "that in year one you recruited one hundred new customers and your average annual retention rate averages 80 percent. By the end of only four years only 51 percent of those 100 customers will still remain (100 x .8 x .8 x .8) ." [3]

   In other words, even with a steady and respectable retention rate of 80 percent, the *half-life* of your customer base, the amount it takes for one half of the customer base to be lost, is only four years—yikes! That's a huge profit drain that cannot be counteracted by recruiting new customers as replacements." [4]

3. **Firms view defecting clients as a lost cause.** Most firms foolishly write off former clients as a lost cause and shift their energies to other supposedly more profitable opportunities.

4. **Firms don't know their clients have defected or are contemplating defection.** Take the case of a partner in a mid-sized law practice that focuses on servicing wealthy high-net worth individuals. A typical client might only seek advice once a year. The billing partner will probably not even notice if he doesn't bill a client in a particular year. When he does pick up the fact, that client may have defected—some two years after the last contact—but it's often too late. By then the client has walked.

HOW TO WIN BACK LOST CLIENTS

Before you start any win-back process you need to:

- Calculate the profit potential of a reactivated relationship, and
- Assess the chances your win-back program will succeed.

Although it's difficult to forecast precisely, you need to plan as detailed a forecast of potential future earnings as you can. It is this figure that will ultimately determine how much money and time you can afford to spend on reactivating the relationship. To assess whether clients represent a good win-back prospect, you must understand why they defected in the first place.

Customer loyalty researchers Strauss and Friege have identified five groups of defectors: (1) intentionally pushed away; (2) unintentionally pushed away; (3) pulled away; (4) bought away; and (5) moved away.[5]

1. **Intentionally pushed away:** not wanted, unprofitable to serve
2. **Unintentionally pushed away:** desirable, but firm's performance does not meet client's expectation
3. **Pulled away:** attracted by competition's superior value proposition
4. **Bought away:** attracted by competitor's low-ball pricing
5. **Moved away:** lost because of changes in location

Strauss and Friege's groupings of defectors can be turned into a useful analytical tool like the one shown in Exhibit 4.1.

EXHIBIT 4.1

Analysis of lost clients

Cause of Defection	No.	Further Action Required
Intentionally pushed away		
Unintentionally pushed away		
Pulled away		
Bought away		
Moved away		
Total		

Skilled detective work is sometimes required to uncover a client's *real* reason for defecting. With an important defection you should:

- Review the account history in detail
- Look for signs of defection in letters and other communications.

HOW TO DETECT AT-RISK CLIENTS

It's very rare for a valuable client to defect without warning you, if you know where to look. Sadly, we ignore most of the early warnings of client discontent.[6]

Exhibit 4.2 lists the warning signals of defection you need to look out for.

EXHIBIT 4.2

Early warning signals of impending defection

Source of Information	Evidence
1. Marketing Data	• Declining fee income • Fall in average size/fee • Increased time between assignments • Client buying reduced number of services
2. Frontline Staff	• Increased complaints • More active competitors
3. Client Survey	• Declining levels of satisfaction • Decline in comparative ratings with competitors • New competitive initiatives
4. Accounts Receivable	• Increased invoice disputes • Increased late payments
5. Loyal Clients	• Specific feedback from loyal clients

Quick Win-Back or Long-Term Win-Back?

With most lost clients you have two choices. Do you go for the quick win-back—usually the moment you discover the client has been lost—or do you concede short-term defeat and plan for a longer term recovery?[7]

QUICK WIN-BACK TACTICS

If you are lucky enough to get the chance to attempt a quick win-back, you must:

- Listen empathetically and prove you really do understand your client's concerns
- Offer a full, immediate, no ifs or buts, comprehensive resolution to the problem
- Make yourself personally accountable and responsible for resolving the problem
- Overcompensate your client. This is not the time to haggle over details—even if you think you are in the right
- Never denigrate the competition they are defecting to. This will simply make your position worse.
- Plan a fall-back strategy. You may not save the whole account, but there may still be a chance to retain a portion of it.
- Depart on good terms and ask if you can stay in contact.

LONG-TERM WIN-BACK

When there's no chance to quickly win back an account, you should position yourself for a comeback and then set about drafting a long-term win-back plan.

To position yourself for a come back make sure you:
Part company on excellent terms, ask for permission to repitch for the client's future work, and ask for permission to stay in touch.

A successful long-term win-back campaign will:

- Acknowledge the value of the lapsed client's past business
- Demonstrate how you've solved the problems that caused the client to leave in the first place

- Show the lapsed client how easy it is for him to restore the relationship
- Offer a fresh, compelling, new value proposition to give the lapsed client an incentive to return
- Offer the lapsed client proof from a reputable third party of how you've improved since you parted company.

Be patient. It takes time—sometimes years—to win back a lapsed client. But remember—it usually costs much less time and money to win back a lapsed client than to close a fresh prospect.

HOW TO SAVE AT-RISK CUSTOMERS

Twenty to 40 percent of typical professional firms' clients are considering defection. Yet the great majority of professional firms we've worked with have no system of identifying clients about to defect.

At-risk clients fall into two groups:

1. Clients who call to terminate their relationship
2. Clients who say nothing but still display many of the tell-tale signs of defection.

The EAR Recovery Formula

To save at-risk customers, think of the EAR recovery formula. EAR is an acronym for a three-step formula you can use to save an at-risk relationship.

The three **EAR** steps are:

1. Empathize to prove you understand the client's problem
2. Ask the client how it wants its problem resolved
3. Respond with a tailored solution.

STEP 1: EMPATHIZE—PROVE YOU UNDERSTAND THE CLIENT'S PROBLEM

To get to the heart of a client's problem, Griffin and Lowenstein say you must uncover three key client needs: the trigger need, the driving need, and original needs.

First, deal with the *trigger need*. The trigger need is the concern that causes the customer to declare, "That's it, I've had enough of this. I'm off."

Here are two useful questions to probe for a client's trigger need:

- Why are you thinking of leaving us?
- I'm truly sorry you're thinking of leaving. Could you please tell me why, so I can put it right.

To successfully address a trigger need, you first have to diffuse the anger that comes packaged with a client's disillusionment.

It is imperative that you:

- Don't interrupt the clients as they vent their anger. And give them time to cool down
- Prove to the clients you really do understand their problems by paraphrasing and clarifying their concerns.

Secondly, deal with the *driving need*. The driving need is the deeper festering set of problems that form the root of the client's discontent. To uncover the driving need, ask:

- What problems have you experienced before?
- If you leave us, where do you plan to go?
- What is it about [competitor's name] that makes them so appealing?

The task here is to uncover what is driving the customer away and give you the information you need to come up with a competitive proposition that might just salvage the account.

Third, stress the *original need*. Since the clients are still full of angst, it pays to remind them why they were attracted to you in the first place. In spite of their frustrations, you may still be a better provider when all factors are considered.

Ask the clients:

- What attracted you to us when you came to us back in [date]?
- Which of our services have you found the most useful? Why?

STEP 2: ASK THE CLIENTS HOW THEY WANT THE PROBLEM RESOLVED

Now that you have uncovered their concerns, you must ask the client what you can do to save the business.

Ask: "What can we do to compensate for all the trouble we've put you to and keep you as a client?"

STEP 3: RESPOND WITH A TAILORED SOLUTION

Finally, your proposal must above all demonstrate that you appreciate the seriousness of the problem your client faces, and you're absolutely committed to putting it right.

This is not the time to come across as petty or mean spirited by making low-cost or illusionary offers. These simply make the defecting client even more determined to leave.

Exit Interview All Important Clients

Whenever you lose an important client, you should conduct a formal exit interview. Most former clients will give an exit interview if approached properly. We've found the best people to conduct exit interviews are former partners or skilled human resource practitioners. Exhibit 4.3 lists the three key issues you need to address in an exit interview.[8]

EXHIBIT 4.3

Questions to ask in an exit interview

Here are three key issues you need to address in an exit interview:

1. Why did you stop using our services?
   - Technical expertise of key staff
   - Ability of staff to give you a competitive edge
   - Quality of the service
   - Quality of our service support
   - Helpfulness and friendliness of our staff
   - Access to senior staff or partner
   - Relationship with senior staff or partner
   - Competitor offered an irresistible price
   - Competitor offered more expertise or better value solution
   - Changed location
   - Badly handled complaint(s)
   - Invoice or billing dispute.

2. Did you share with us your concerns before you decided to stop using us?

3. What do we need to do for you to consider using us again?

ACTION

STEPS

1. Develop a win-back program to recover at-risk and lost clients.

2. Set up measures to record and calculate:
   - Number of lost clients
   - Percent of clients who defect
   - Potential lost revenues as a result of defections
   - Numbers of lost clients regained
   - Percent of lapsed clients recovered
   - Dollar value of your win-back campaigns.

3. Develop early warning system to detect when clients are at risk of defecting.

4. Design an at-risk profile based on an analysis of past lost clients.

5. Conduct exit interviews with all lost top tier clients.

6. Conduct defection interviews with representative cross-section of lost clients.

7. Train selected staff on how to save at-risk and defecting clients.

8. Draft a long-term win-back program to win back lapsed clients.

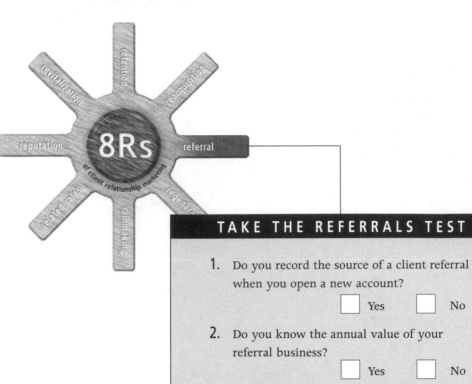

8Rs of client relationship marketing

revitalization · retention · reacquisition · referral · regeneration · rainmaking · related sales · reputation

1. Do you record the source of a client referral when you open a new account?

   ☐ Yes ☐ No

2. Do you know the annual value of your referral business?

   ☐ Yes ☐ No

3. Can you quickly identify your top ten referral sources?

   ☐ Yes ☐ No

4. Do you actively cultivate referrals among your existing clients?

   ☐ Yes ☐ No

5. Do you have a reward or recognition program designed to maintain and grow your referral business?

   ☐ Yes ☐ No

6. Do you calculate the referral value of the community or business networks you belong to?

   ☐ Yes ☐ No

7. Do you explicitly identify and cultivate the most "influential" referral sources in the community or business networks you belong to? Value of each of your clients?

   ☐ Yes ☐ No

CHAPTER 5

REFERRALS

How to woo low cost prospects by networking with the right people

Features

- The economics of referral business
- Becoming an angler
- Working a room for profit
- How to get referrals from existing clients
- How to start a referral network from scratch
- Putting a formal referral marketing system in place
- Winning referrals from fellow professionals
- The hierarchy of networking
- Turning your alumni into a high value referral network
- Action steps

THE ECONOMICS OF REFERRAL BUSINESS

Referrals represent the most profitable source of new business for most professional firms. It costs much less to close a referred prospect. Our research with a small sample of accounting firms suggests it costs approximately 400 percent more to close an unreferred prospect than a referred prospect.

It takes much less time to close a referred prospect. It takes approximately half the time to close a referred prospect than it does to sell to a nonreferred prospect.

Referred prospects are much more likely to be loyal. People who purchase as a result of a personal referral are more likely to be loyal than clients who buy because of a price promotion.

EXHIBIT 5.1

Acquisition costs for referred clients are lower

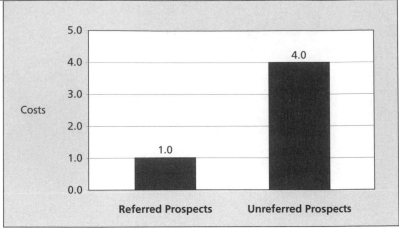

Mills Group Client Research.

The odds of closing a referred prospect are substantially higher than a nonreferred prospect. Research on U.S. Middle Bank customers, for example, shows the odds of closing a referred prospect are 83 percent. That compares with odds of 49 percent for nonreferred prospects.

Referrals work because they come from an unbiased second party. The recommendation comes from someone within your network of contacts who knows you and your services and has faith in your ability to follow through.

As a result, the profit contribution of referrals to a professional practice can be remarkably high.

The Mathematics of Networking

Networking works like compound interest. Professional services consultant and author Ford Harding says, "the value of a network of market contacts is worth more than the sum of its parts and that value grows geometrically with the size of the network."[1]

A professional who has 500 people in her network can make 124,750 matches. A professional with 1,500 network contacts has more than one million possible matches.

The Sources of Referrals

In *The World's Best Known Marketing Secret: Building Your Business With Word-of-Mouth Marketing,* Ivan Misner describes six types of networking groups that generate business referrals:

- **Casual-contact networks**—general business groups, such as the Chambers of Commerce that allow people from various overlapping professions
- **Strong-contact networks**—groups that allow only one member per profession and that meet weekly to exchange leads
- **Community service clubs**—groups like Rotary and Kiwanis, which exist primarily to serve the community but which are also a good source of referrals
- **Professional associations**—groups of people in a single industry or profession whose primary purpose is to exchange information and ideas
- **Social/business groups**—dual purpose organizations such as the Jaycees that combine business with pleasure, with emphasis on the latter
- **Women's business organizations**—relatively recent networking groups paralleling the "old-boy networks" that formerly excluded females.[2]

Remember, not all networks are equal. The most profitable networks are those made up of people who share common business concerns or problems.

BECOMING AN ANGLER

Master networkers think like anglers. "The Angler," writes master networker and author Elisabeth L. Misner, "goes looking for a particular kind of fish; he knows where it is likely to be found and what kind of bait to use. He knows you can't just throw your line in any puddle and expect a strike. To be an Angler you have to plan ahead, research your quarry, look in the right places, and shut out all distractions. Once he's found the fish he's looking for, the Angler reels it in patiently and by practicing 'gives gain'—the cultivation of mutual benefits."[3]

Fifteen Ways to Use Your Network

To make your network work, you need to appreciate precisely what each member in your network can do for you.

Authors and networking authorities Ivan Misner and Robert Davis[4] have identified fifteen ways network members can help you. Your network sources can:

1. Exhibit your brochures and marketing materials
2. Distribute your promotional materials
3. Increase your visibility at an event by publicly endorsing an event you are promoting
4. Invite you to their events, programs, and seminars
5. Endorse your services by publicly singing your praises
6. Nominate you for recognition and awards
7. Supply you with leads
8. Provide you with referrals
9. Make the initial contact for you with prospects
10. Introduce you to prospects
11. Arrange a meeting on your behalf
12. Follow up with prospects they referred to you and provide additional reassurance
13. Print information about you in their publications
14. Sponsor a program you are hosting
15. Actively sell your services by persuading a prospect to buy from you

Search for Problems

For networking to succeed, you must be one of the first people they think of when they face the type of problems you can solve. This means your contacts must know and appreciate what services you and your firm provide. Contacts have to think of you when they confront a need for the services your firm sells.

Successful networkers find ways of continually reminding their network what problems they solve and what services they provide.

WORKING A ROOM FOR PROFIT

Most professionals go to networking events, but few know how to network successfully. Most professionals confuse networking with socializing. Here are the fundamental do's and don'ts.

- Review the guest list if you can. Target whom you want to talk to and set specific call objectives. Check if someone else from your firm should also go.
- Turn up early with your cards, ready to work the room.
- Eat early. It's hard to eat, shake hands, talk, and work a room with a plate of food in hand.
- If you go with a colleague, split up. You achieve much more working alone.
- Walk the room first. Surveying the room lets you target and prioritize your calls.
- Rehearse your 30 second personal introduction. In less than 30 seconds you must be able to differentiate yourself, differentiate your work or approach, and differentiate your firm.
- Move on if the person doesn't represent a good prospect.
- Use positive body talk. Use a firm handshake, and smile and stand with an open posture.
- Don't sell. The purpose is to establish your credibility and set up an appointment; nothing more, nothing less.
- Spend most of your time with people you don't know. This is not the place to gossip with friends and colleagues.
- Spend the rest of the time cementing existing relationships. Use this time to strengthen the loyalty bond between you and your firm.
- Sequence your conversation:
  - Introduce yourself (5 to 10 seconds)
  - Discover what the prospect does (1 to 3 minutes)

- Talk about common interests (1 to 2 minutes)
- Arouse interest in your service (30 seconds)
- Deepen rapport by finding common ground (1 to 2 minutes)
- Exchange cards. Give your card first. (Offer a reward. "If you give me your card I'll send you an article on...")
- Write action points on the back of the card or note them in your pocket or electronic diary
- Move on to the next prospect once you've confirmed your next action (mail, call, appointment).
- Work the entire room. Allow 5 minutes for a marginal prospect, 10 minutes for a promising prospect, 20 minutes for a top prospect.

Compile a Patterned Sequence of Questions

Bob Burg, author of the bestselling *Endless Referrals,* has turned referral marketing into an art. To get the prospects talking about their problems, you need to develop a patterned sequence of questions.

Here are Bob Burg's top ten questions.

1. How did you get started in the networking business?
2. What was the biggest challenge you had to overcome?
3. What distinguishes you and your company from your competitors?
4. What advice would you give someone just starting in the widgit business?
5. What one thing would you do with your business if you knew you could not fail?
6. What are the biggest changes that have affected your business?
7. What do you see as the coming trends in your business?
8. Describe the funniest or strangest incident you've experienced in business.
9. What ways have you found the most effective for promoting your business?
10. What one sentence would you like people to use in describing the way you do business?[5]

How to Get Referrals from Existing Clients

Lots of professionals get gun shy when it comes to asking an existing client for referrals. They don't know when or how to ask. When to ask for a referral depends on the nature of your profession. In general, the best time to ask is straight after you have completed work that has delighted the client.

The best way to ask for a referral is to:

- Tell your clients how much you enjoyed working with them—suggest they should probably mix with other people like themselves who share their values and attitudes to service and performance.
- Explain you're trying to build your business around clients who share the same values and concerns—ask who they know would benefit from the same types of services you provide.
- Paint a profile of the types of clients who you believe would benefit most from your services.
- Tell the client the ideal referral is probably someone who has experienced dissatisfaction with his existing provider.
- Ask them for specific names.
- Promise to call the referral within 24 hours of talking to your prospect. And check that it is okay to use his name.

JOIN MULTIPLE NETWORKING GROUPS

If you're serious about networking, you must join more than one networking group. It's very rare for professionals who primarily rely on referral business to find one group or type of group is enough.

How to Start a Referral Network from Scratch

Every professional service firm should maintain a database of networking contacts. If you don't have a formal database of networking contacts, you should start compiling one by answering the questions below. Ask:

1. Who has supplied me with leads in the past?
2. Who sells to the same people as I do?
3. Who buys from the same people as I do?
4. Who successfully networks with my top clients?
5. Whom do my top competitors network with?
6. Who would benefit most from my help, endorsement, or recommendation?

Once you have a large list of names, you need to categorize into groups based on their potential networking value to you. To identify potential networking groups complete Exhibit 5.2. Start by compiling a profile of the ideal prospect. Then list the various groups where you're likely to find large numbers of your ideal prospect.

EXHIBIT 5.2

Identifying potential networking groups

Ideal Prospect	Trade/Business Professional Organizations	Community/ Service Clubs	Social/Sporting/ Cultural Groups
Occupation:			
Industry:			
Age:			
Gender:			
Income:			
Education:			
Interests:			

PUTTING A FORMAL REFERRAL MARKETING SYSTEM IN PLACE

For referral marketing to work, you need a formal referral system that consistently and systematically generates the supply of referrals you need to grow and prosper. Exhibit 5.3 highlights the information you need to collect when tracking the source of referrals.

EXHIBIT 5.3

Referral Tracking

Rank	Name	Number of Referrals This Period	Converted Referrals	Conversion Ratio*	Total Referrals Sales
1					
2					
3					
4					
5					
6					
7					
8					
9					
10					

*Low referral sales value may be offset by high conversion rate.

WINNING REFERRALS FROM FELLOW PROFESSIONALS

Referrals for many professionals come from within their own profession or a closely related one. Lawyers, for example, commonly refer work to each other. Some engineers are heavily dependent on referrals from architects. This type of referral needs to be cultivated, monitored, and measured.

EXHIBIT 5.4

Referrals from fellow professionals

Referral Name	Firm	Speciality	Relation/ship (1–4)*	Fee Potential **

*Relationship
1 = excellent
2 = good
3 = weak
4 = nonexistent

** Fee Potential
H = high
M = medium
L = low

Because of the importance of referrals from fellow professionals, you should also keep a separate file for each referral source. Exhibit 5.5 shows the data you need to collect.

EXHIBIT 5.5

Referral information

Name:	Firm:
Speciality:	Current Relationship:
Quality of Referrals:	Fee Potential:
Outside Interests:	Professional Affiliations:

Plans for Enhancing Relationship:

Relationship	Quality of Referrals	Fee Potential
1 = excellent	H = high	H = high
2 = good	M = medium	M = medium
3 = weak	L = low	L = low
4 = nonexistent		

THE HIERARCHY OF NETWORKING

When forming relationships with networks, you need to understand the *hierarchy of networking*. "For marketers, the more exclusive and successful an association's membership, the more attractive it is," says John Warrillow, author of *Drilling for Gold*.[6]

EXHIBIT 5.6

Hierarchy of small business associations

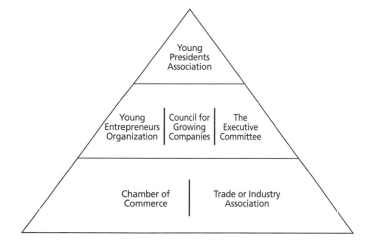

Take the small business market, for example. At the bottom of the pyramid are the Chambers of Commerce. These are the easiest associations to join. The next level includes groups such as the Young Entrepreneurs Organization (YEO) and the Council for Growing Companies. These have more restrictive memberships. At the top of small business networks is the Young Presidents Association (YPA). Members of the YPA members must be under 50 and have at least fifty full-time employees.

The higher you go, the more valuable and more targeted the group.

TURNING YOUR ALUMNI INTO A HIGH VALUE REFERRAL NETWORK

The best professional services firms treat their former staff like alumni—because they know that former staff are one of the best sources of referral work. Former staff are highly influential reference sources about your firms' capabilities. The best professional firms such as McKinsey know this, and develop sophisticated alumni programs for their staff.

McKinsey's network of alumni of more than 10,000 is so influential, that the *Sunday Business Times* calls the McKinsey network "a mutually enforcing brotherhood." The network is a fabulous marketing machine and a machine many of its rivals would like to replicate," reports Matthew Lynn of the *Sunday Business Times*.[7] When you appreciate the astonishing number of CEOs who have come from McKinsey, you begin to appreciate the value of the network. Lou Gerstner, the recently retired CEO of IBM, is just one of many CEOs who have come from what *Fortune* magazine calls the McKinsey CEO factory.[8] Have no doubt— alumni referrals are enormously profitable. We estimate 30 percent of McKinsey's work comes from its alumni network.[9]

According to Cem Sertoglu and Anne Berkowitch, the CEO and vice president of *Select Minds,* a New York–based alumni relations management company, the best alumni programs are built on three foundations:

1. *An enlightened exit process.* Staff must leave on good terms and be sold on the value of staying in touch.
2. *A two-way value proposition.* Former employees need to have an incentive to keep in contact. "It's not enough to send alumni newsletters. The most effective alumni programs offer additional benefits, such as access to semi-proprietary intellectual capital, free or subsidized training programs, and invitations to events and social gatherings," say Sertoglu and Berkowitch.[10]
3. *Personalized communications.* Where possible, firms personalize and tailor messages to their former colleagues. "What a retired senior vice president wants to hear and learn is probably different from what an old associate who has gone back to school for an MBA is interested in."[11]

1. Establish a formal database of networking contacts.

2. Put in place a formal system to track all the work that comes from referrals.

3. Prepare a formal referral marketing plan for each specialty area.

4. Consider the advantages of establishing a formal alumni marketing program.

5. Assign each professional specific referral marketing goals.

6. Train all your professionals on "how to work a room."

8Rs

revitalization · regeneration · reacquisition · retention · referral · reputation · related sales · *of client relationship marketing*

TAKE THE REGENERATION TEST

1. Do you target specific market segments and niches to dominate?

   ☐ Yes   ☐ No

2. Do you use small group seminars with prospects and clients as a vehicle for attracting valuable prospects?

   ☐ Yes   ☐ No

3. Do you have a formal publicity strategy?

   ☐ Yes   ☐ No

4. Are any of your practice experts regularly quoted by the media as an "expert news source"?

   ☐ Yes   ☐ No

5. Do you use direct mail or e-mail marketing to generate quality prospects?

   ☐ Yes   ☐ No

6. Do you use newsletters as a marketing vehicle to promote your services?

   ☐ Yes   ☐ No

7. Have you moved your newsletters from "snail mail" to "e-mail"?

   ☐ Yes   ☐ No

CHAPTER 6

REGENERATION

How to rebuild and grow your client base by targeting the right markets

Features

- Targeting high profit prospects
- Targeting a single segment
- Attracting prospects with seminars
- Persuasive public speaking
- Wowing with visual aids
- Using smart PR to generate free publicity
- Becoming an expert news source
- Writing influential articles
- The power of direct mail
- E-mail marketing that sells
- Marketing with client newsletters
- Moving to e-mail newsletters
- Advertising for results
- Action steps

TARGETING HIGH PROFIT PROSPECTS

Ongoing client attrition means that you must constantly be regenerating and rebuilding your client base with fresh prospects. The most profitable firms target their prospects with pinpoint precision.

When notorious bank robber Willy Sutton was asked why he robbed banks, he replied, "Because that's where the money is."

Successful rainmaking firms:
- Target the right prospects
- Learn to recognize and reject the wrong prospects
- Develop their services with your best clients' needs in mind
- Staff their firm with talent to match their best clients' needs.

TARGET THE RIGHT PROSPECTS

To attract the right prospects, you must answer four key questions:

1. What are our core competencies? How you define your specialties and expertise will largely determine the type of customers you attract.
2. What categories of clients and industries can we offer the most value? Some groups of clients and some industries are inherently more profitable.
3. What groups of clients match our minimum fee and profit expectations? You must include minimum profit and minimum fee requirements when you define your target clients.
4. What are the odds of repeat business? The best prospects are usually those whom you can grow with repeat work.

LEARN TO RECOGNIZE AND REJECT THE WRONG PROSPECTS

Learn how to recognize prospects you need to avoid. Refusing to consider and turning away bad business are critical if you want business growth and have a profitable practice.

Watch out for and avoid:

- *Price grinders.* Avoid prospects that demand an initial low price and in return promise lots of future work.
- *Chronic defectors.* Clients who regularly change professional service providers always represent trouble and are impossible to satisfy.
- *Discourteous jerks.* Don't do business with rude, abusive clients. Life's too short.
- *Misfits.* Avoid clients whose needs aren't a match with your capabilities.

Always be selective when you sell to new prospects. Keep in mind marketing strategist David Siegel's advice: "Remember, the customer is always right, but not all customers are always right for you."[1]

DEVELOP YOUR SERVICES WITH YOUR BEST CLIENTS IN MIND

Most professional providers adapt their core services to meet the needs of their best clients by providing add-ons. This incremental approach will rarely give you the competitive edge you need to lock in these clients for long-term profitable sustainable growth. Smart top professional firms often find the most successful and profitable services are those conceived from the beginning with the best clients in mind.

Designing products and services from scratch with particular groups in mind enables you to optimize the value you can deliver to a client. And as you optimize the value to your client, you can optimize your fee.

Montana-based consulting firm Anderson, Zurnuehlen and Company installs client server and SQL Accounting software. In 1994, it began developing a standardized approach aimed at the needs of a sophisticated set of clients.

Because their value proposition has been developed with a specific set of clients in mind, Anderson Zurnuehlen will not accept a client who does not meet their strict selection criteria. Their ten selection criteria include a willingness to take advice, recognition and payment for quality service, reasonable expectations, good profitability, and strong industry position.

As a result, the average size fee has gone up from $9,000 to $50,000, and profits have jumped from 25 percent to 30 percent of gross revenues.[2]

STAFF YOUR FIRM TO MATCH YOUR BEST CLIENTS' NEEDS

One of the biggest constraints in growing your top 20 percent of clients is often a lack of staff who have the talents and credibility to work on a sophisticated, demanding client's file. Hard decisions have to be made. If you have staff whose skill set can't meet your best clients' needs and you don't have profitable alternative work, get rid of these staff members. Then consciously start recruiting staff with skill and personality profiles that match the expectations of your best clients. And watch your practice grow.

THE SIX FOCUS STRATEGIES

Superior profits come from disciplined focus—a disciplined focus is about providing superior value to a highly targeted niche group of customers.

No professional service firm can keep up to date, let alone ahead, with all the changes in all of its markets. Even the Big Four, with tens of thousands of staff and offices on virtually every continent, struggle to provide a one-stop shop across multiple service lines in multiple geographies. Focusing on the services you excel in will lower operating costs, increase customer loyalty, and raise profits.

U.S. Services marketing professors Craig Terrill and Arthur Middlebrooks have found success starts with focus and *"learning to say no."* They have identified six strategies to help you focus your practice.

1. Lines of business focus
2. Service focus
3. Benefits focus
4. Geography focus
5. Channel focus
6. Customer type focus.[3]

LINES OF BUSINESS FOCUS

The first strategy? Narrow the lines of businesses or markets you serve. Industry and market specialization lowers internal costs. Have no doubt—clients will pay a premium for staff and businesses who provide genuine industry expertise.

One of the first and most critical questions clients ask when choosing a professional service provider is, "What industry expertise do you have?" or "Whom else have you worked for in our line of business?"

Have you ever tried to promote a new professional service across multiple markets and businesses? It's difficult, time consuming, and costly. Marketing a message with an industry focus is much easier and often much more profitable. You can run an industry-based seminar, write an article for the industry journal; you can speak at an industry conference; or act as an industry commentator for the broader business press. Marketing synergy also comes when you can deliver the same message to the same group in multiple ways.

SERVICE FOCUS

The second strategy? Become a service specialist and offer a narrow but select menu.

There are two ways to profit from a service specialization strategy: The first way is to become an expert—a specialist in your field—and charge a price premium for your services. For example, a tax expert on company takeovers can usually charge a much higher premium than a general tax accountant.

Service specialization is a proven strategy. Generalized services are much more likely to suffer from commodification and discounting.

The second way to increase profits from offering a limited service menu is to "cherry pick" the high-profit margin services. In a number of professional service areas, providers earn good profits on simple routine activities that they sometimes use to subsidize the less routine, more complex, less predictable diagnoses.

The potential exists for a professional service entrepreneur to offer a streamlined service, a limited menu of routine services at a substantial discount.

BENEFITS FOCUS

The third strategy? Sell a unique package of benefits that can be leveraged across a large number of clients. The key here is to create a unique bundle of benefits that is proprietary or is, at the very least, difficult to copy.

GEOGRAPHY FOCUS

The fourth focus strategy? Concentrate on your local market, be it city, region, or even country.

Despite the fact that technology has shrunk the world to a global village and global firms can and do move teams of professionals from Atlanta to Jakarta at a week's notice, geographic focus remains highly viable. Why? Clients remain distinctively different in many markets. Decisions for many types of professional services are still made locally. Locally owned and operated companies are consciously preferred in some areas. Many professional service firms find the costs of serving and marketing to local clients much lower.

CHANNEL FOCUS

The fifth strategy? Limit channel access.

Clients can typically access professional service providers through multiple access channels: face-to-face, telephone, e-mail, Internet, fax, and video conferencing. Because client behaviors and expectations vary between channels, it is possible to offer services specifically tailored to a particular channel.

In a number of countries, tax experts provide low-cost, online, and phone advice to sole practitioners who don't want to bother with a face-to-face session for a full opinion.

The U.S.–based law firm visalaw.com, started by Greg Siskind, has been enormously successful selling specialist legal immigration advice via the Web. The firm offers services by providing online assistance to clients all over the world looking for advice on immigrating to America.

CUSTOMER TYPE FOCUS

The sixth and last focus strategy? Focus on the types of clients you can serve profitably.

Picking the right client and sidestepping the wrong client to serve is the key to every focus strategy. The goal is to find groups of underserved clients that match your skills and talents.

How to Use the Six Focus Strategies

As you assess each of the six focus strategies, remember that success comes from *working multiple strategies in tandem*.

Once you have chosen the prime focus strategies you wish to choose, ask:

- Which market niches should we go after?
- Which niches should we avoid?

Never forget that the primary goal is to pinpoint highly profitable niches you can dominate. These niches will provide your best sources of gold and silver clients.

EXHIBIT 6.1

Focus strategies

Strategy	Advantages	Disadvantages	✔	✘
Lines of business focus				
Service focus				
Benefits focus				
Geographic focus				
Customer focus				
Channel focus				

Become the Supplier of First Choice

The most ambitious—and usually the most profitable—professional service firms follow an explicit strategy: *Become the supplier of first choice in the most profitable segments.* Leadership in most professional service market segments means you can command a price premium—at least 20 percent in prosperous times. And in a recession or declining market, the market leader can much more easily resist discount pressures.

Here is a five-step process on how to identify and dominate profitable markets based on the work of service marketing experts Craig Terrill and Arthur Middlebrooks.[4]

To segment your clients you need to follow a five-step process:
Step 1: Identify key client needs, attitudes, behaviors, and demographics
Step 2: Group clients into segments with like buying habits
Step 3: Profile each distinctive segment
Step 4: Size each segment for potential revenues and profits
Step 5: Target the most attractive segments

Step 1: Identify Key Client Needs, Attitudes, Behaviors, and Demographics

ASSESSING CLIENT NEEDS

Client needs vary enormously. But a useful place to start is to ask two questions:

- How complex are the client's needs?
- How important is our service to the client's business or work?

Clients with complex needs present lots of opportunities for providers to create highly differentiated services.

Clients who rate your service as highly important to their business success have a strong incentive to develop an intimate relationship with a provider and develop an in-depth appreciation of what a sophisticated provider can deliver.

ASSESSING CLIENT ATTITUDES

Client beliefs and preferences can provide valuable insights. In particular, look for evidence on the way clients commission services. Some clients are essentially *reactive* or event driven. They wait until a problem occurs before they take action. Other clients are *proactive*. They spend time and money on preventative activities to avoid the problem occurring in the first place.

So when you assess client attitudes, ask, are they "proactive" or "reactive"? Look for evidence on how they form relationships with suppliers. Some clients treat their suppliers as vendors and choose largely on price. Others treat their suppliers as partners.

OBSERVING CLIENT BEHAVIORS

Behaviors are past actions customers have taken that can be observed, tracked, and measured. Remember: *Past behaviors are the best indicators of future buying behavior.*

The behaviors you might typically encounter include:
- A preference to do work wherever possible "in-house" versus "outsource"
- The types of services purchased in the past
- The providers of past services
- The pattern of spending on various services
- Loyalty toward particular suppliers
- Membership in key trade associations
- Subscriptions to key trade magazines.

CLIENT DEMOGRAPHICS

Demographic information allows you to classify and categorize your clients under a variety of useful headings.

In businesses, these typically include:
- The size of company profits
- The industry classification of the business
- The number of employees

For individuals the key variables are:

- Net worth
- Geographic location
- Income level
- Occupation

EXHIBIT 6.2

Client needs/ attitudes/ behaviors/ demographics

Needs Complexity Importance (high, low) Complexity (high, low)	
Commissioning of Services Proactive? Reactive?	
Relationship with Suppliers Vendor/price driven? Partner/value driven?	
Work Control In-house? Outsource?	
Past Service Providers List names	
Loyalty to Suppliers Relationship driven? Transaction driven?	
Key Trade Associations List	
Reading List trade magazines	
Business Demographics Industry Classification No. Company profits (Last 3 years) No. of employees	
Individual Demographics Occupation Net worth Annual income Location	

Step 2: Group Clients into Segments with Like Buying Habits

The second step is to analyze the information you gathered on client needs, attitudes, behaviors, and demographics, looking for similar patterns among groups in the way they buy.

Typically, three variables account for most of the differences between the low- and high-profit segments:

- Their risk posture
- Complexity of needs
- Price sensitivity

Risk stance: Risk-averse clients are worriers. They like to have their hands held. Risk acceptors are prepared to do the work in-house.

Complexity of needs: Clients with complex needs tend to look for service providers who can provide close, intimate support. Clients with simple needs usually don't need hand holders.

Price sensitivity: Transaction-driven clients treat their suppliers as vendors. Relationship-driven clients usually put the value of the partnership before the price.

EXHIBIT 6.3

Group buying habits

Risk Stance
     Risk averse?
     Risk acceptors?	

Complexity of Needs
     Simple needs?
     Complex needs?	

Price Sensitivity
     Transaction driven?
     Relationship driven?	

Step 3: Profile Each Distinctive Segment

We should now be able to create a segment profile that describes what a typical client looks like (Exhibit 6.4).

A segment profile will normally include:

- Critical client needs
- Decision-making process
- Purchase criteria
- Your reputation
- Key competitor's reputation
- Usage patterns
- Loyalty to suppliers
- Key demographics

EXHIBIT 6.4

Segment profile

Critical client needs List and rank 1–5	
Decision-making process Describe	
Purchase criteria List and rank	
Your reputation Credibility in segment	
Key competitor's reputation Credibility in segment	
Usage patterns Heavy, medium, light, nonusers	
Loyalty to suppliers Transaction-driven? Relationship-driven?	
Key demographics: **Industry** 　Revenue 　Profits 　Employees **Individuals** 　Income 　Occupation 　Location	

Step 4: Size Each Segment for Revenues and Profits

There is no point in chasing a sector that is too small or lacks the growth potential to ever become profitable.

Segment size depends on five factors:

1. **The number of potential clients in each segment.** Multiple clients represent multiple opportunities.

2. **The annual revenue potential of each segment.** To calculate the total dollar spend, multiply the average annual spend per customer in a segment by the total number of clients in the segment. The annual spend can vary enormously from year to year, especially in markets that are naturally highly cyclical, and you may need to estimate an average spend.

3. **The profit potential of each segment.** Profits per customer vary enormously between sectors and depend on:
   - Price sensitivity
   - Cost to serve
   - The average size of a purchase.

4. **Segment growth.** It is much easier to grow if the market in which your client is operating is also growing.

5. **The potential revenues from new services.** This is highly speculative, but certain segments such as IT are inherently more receptive to new offerings.

Step 5: Target the Most Attractive Segments

Few professional firms have the resources to chase business in all the profitable segments they identify. The obvious strategy and invariably the most lucrative is to focus on the most attractive segments. Market attractiveness is largely determined by eight factors (see Exhibit 6.6):

1. **The size of the market.** Big markets offer more chances to grow. For large professional service firms large markets are

EXHIBIT 6.5

Market size

Potential Clients Total number	
Annual Revenue Potential Average annual % growth over 3 years	
Segment Profit Potential Price sensitivity Cost to serve Average size of purchase	
Segment Growth Trend Growing, flat, declining? Estimate %	
Potential Revenue from New Services Estimate	

essential for growth. Large markets also offer smaller firms profitable niches. Remember the adage that there are "riches in niches."

2. **Growth potential.** It is much easier to grow if your client's markets are buoyant and growing. A clients market that is growing at 10 percent per annum will double in size in eight years.

3. **Competitive intensity.** Research shows the most important driver of profitability in a market is competitive intensity. It is always difficult to crack markets that already have a number of strong aggressive players.

4. **Profit potential.** Potential profits have to be high enough to make a segment attractive enough. When estimating potential profits play conservative. Take your most pessimistic estimate of profits and then slice another 20 percent off the figure.

5. **Strategic direction.** The segment you are considering entering should fit with your strategic direction and identity.

6. **Capabilities.** You need the technical and operational capacity to serve the segment. Building new skill sets to tackle a new market is expensive and risky.

7. **The cyclicity of the market.** Some client businesses are highly cyclical—the way and pattern of purchase of professional services is highly influenced by the stage in the industry cycle. Any accounting firm that sells insolvency services knows it will have to live with troughs in demand typically when times are prosperous.

8. **Risk factors.** Some markets face significant and predictable downside risks. These vary enormously but include political stability, monetary conditions, regularity in climate, and tax changes. Whatever they are, you need to factor them in.

EXHIBIT 6.6

Market attractiveness

Market Size Estimate	
Growth Potential High, medium, low Estimate % growth	
Competitive Intensity High, medium, low	
Profit Potential High, medium, low Specify margins	
Strategic Direction Ideal, reasonable, poor fit	
Capabilities Match Describe current	
Market Cyclicity Describe patterns or cycles	
Risk Factors List and rank	
Overall Attractiveness Very attractive, attractive, or unattractive	

TARGETING A SINGLE SEGMENT | In some markets, the most profitable strategy can be to concentrate on a single segment. "Single segment market offers three advantages," says marketing professor and author Philip Kotler.[5]

1. You can more easily identify the buyer in the segment, meet them, run focus groups, and design tailored offerings.
2. There are fewer competitors to identify and track in a well-defined segment.
3. The odds of becoming the "supplier of choice" are much greater in a single segment. Being recognized as the "supplier of choice" normally means you can increase your market share and margin at the same time.

There Are Riches in Niches

Analyze the profitability and income streams in a professional firm, and it is remarkable how often the super profits come from highly profitable niches.

According to Kotler, "niches describe smaller sets of customers who have more narrowly defined needs [than a segment] or unique combinations of needs."[6]

Niche specialization allows you to create superior profits by focusing on the few things you do extraordinarily well for a highly targeted group of clients.

Niche specialization means you really can get to know each client intimately. In a niche there usually are fewer competitors to watch. The higher margins that result from niche specialization come from clients who are willing to pay for the added expertise niche specialists offer.

A fan of niche marketing, Kotler warns, "you have to watch a niche doesn't become a pothole."[7] The smart approach is to spread your risks by pursuing a *multiniche* strategy.

For obvious reasons, professional firms don't like publicly sharing information about their profitable niches, but there is compelling evidence there are "riches in niches."

In his remarkably insightful book *Hidden Champions,*[8] Herman Simon lists a long list of virtually unknown German companies that earn solid profits by niche specialization. Simon's list, which is limited to companies that hold more than 50 percent of the world market share in their niches, includes such names as Steiner Optical, which holds 80 percent of the world's military field glasses market.

Simon reports his hidden champions' success comes from superior performance combined with highly responsive customer service, direct and regular contact by management with key customers, and relentless innovation aimed at improving customer value.

Simon's hidden champions' success formula mirrors that of the highly successful professional service firm niche players.

Crosslin, Slaten & O'Connor—The Bug Lawyers

In 1999, two-year old, full-service law firm, Crosslin, Slaten & O'Connor was ready to attempt its first strategic marketing initiative. CS&O wanted to differentiate itself. Rather than trying to build the firm's name recognition within the broad business community, the firm aimed the marketing efforts toward a fast-growth industry where they had significant experience, pest control.

Leveraging the firm's extraordinary industry knowledge, Ross Rishman Marketing developed the nation's first full-service "Bug Law" practice, one which encompassed all of the firm's practice areas, from litigation to tax, corporate, regulatory, real and estate planning.

The marketing program features:
- Humorous ads in industry trade magazines
- A "We Know Pest Control" brochure

- www.buglaw.com website, with a termite crawling around the home page
- A toll-free 877/BUG-LAW1 phone number
- "Bug 1," the firm's twin-engine airplane.

As a result, in the first year the firm's pest control revenue doubled, the firm developed a national industry reputation, and the firm appeared in a dozen feature articles from the U.S. to the U.K.[9]

ATTRACTING PROSPECTS WITH SEMINARS

Once you've targeted a group of potentially profitable prospects, you have to woo them. Running small group seminars is arguably the most effective way of impressing high quality prospects.

WHY ARE SEMINARS SUCH A GREAT MARKETING TOOL?

Seminars can be highly profitable marketing tools because they:

- Get your name in front of prospective clients
- Allow you to showcase your expertise
- Provide you with name recognition
- Position you as an authority in your chosen field
- Give you face-to-face opportunities to turn prospects into clients
- Are arguably the most effective way of generating high quality business.

SMALL GROUP VS. BALLROOM SEMINARS

By far the most effective seminars are small group (6 to 15 people) functions. The least effective are the large-scale ballroom seminars often delivered by speakers selected from competing firms.

Don't participate in a large-scale seminar unless you can control the topics, or influence the agenda, or there is a compelling strategic reason to participate.

Small group seminars work because you can:

- Invite a qualified, targeted group of prospects
- Focus your presentation on a topic or a problem that you know your audience shares
- Take the time to discuss the concerns of each one of the participants.

THE IDEAL SEMINAR TOPIC

Topic selection is critical to the success of a small group seminar. First ask yourself, *"Is this topic on a problem that I can turn into a need for my services?"* If the topic can't be converted into a need, choose a different topic. The ideal topic is on a problem that is large, complex, and requires urgent action.

Large problems have the potential to be turned into large fees. A useful question to ask when considering what topic to present is how large a problem this is in dollar terms to each of the potential clients I want to invite to my seminar. If the dollar value of the problem you want to talk about is not at least five times the minimum fee you would need to generate profitable work, consider changing the topic.

Complex problems are ideal seminar topics, since complex problems usually require outside expertise to solve.

Urgent problems are ideal since they can be quickly converted into work. Urgent problems are usually far less fee-sensitive and less likely to be put to competitive bidding.

SOME FINAL POINTERS

Don't invite prospects who are competitors to the same seminar. Participants will clam up and rob you of the opportunity to turn their problems into a need for your services.

If you are running a series of seminars, start with the least important group. This will allow you to iron out any teething problems and fine-tune your presentation.

If the seminar topic proves popular and has enduring appeal, consider turning it into a chargeable seminar with supporting videos or audiotapes. These have proved extraordinarily profitable sources of income for some professionals. When this happens marketing suddenly turns from a cost into a revenue stream.

Seminar Guidelines

Kevin Brown of Kevin Brown Marketing, a California-based specialist in professional services marketing, has compiled a ten-point checklist for obtaining new clients from a seminar[10]:

1. Plan way ahead. As many as 120 days are needed to plan and promote a successful seminar.
2. Analyze your targeted market. Find out what prospective clients are looking for.
3. Pick a partner if you think you lack the necessary drawing power.
4. Carefully design the seminar content. Make your presentation content rich; make it worth their time.
5. Promote it effectively. You may need to send several mailings. You are likely to have a response rate of 3–5 percent if you are working with a good database.
   You need to have a title that is catchy, timely, a play on words, or humorous to stand out from the crowd of boring, legalistic sounding titles. You may want to invest in well-placed ads and news releases to promote the event. Good promotion also includes having a table at the seminar with sales materials available to attendees. Lastly, reminder phone calls the day prior to the event have been known to increase attendance by as much as 25 percent.
6. Coach your speakers. A good rule of thumb is that it takes 8 to 10 hours of coaching to put on a good, professional presentation.
7. Prepare visual aids. Have the presenters practice using them. A well-prepared PowerPoint presentation can be very effective.

8. Develop quality handout materials. This is another valuable opportunity to shine.
9. Execute all the logistical details. Dot all the "I"s and cross the "T"s. Make sure there is adequate parking, that the presentation room is cool/warm enough and has proper lighting, and don't let the refreshments run out.
10. Follow up on all possible leads, within 48 hours.

PERSUASIVE PUBLIC SPEAKING

Public speaking helps build your reputation as an expert. A good speaker can generate a dozen or more leads from a good speech delivered to the right audience. Experts who are good speakers can earn sizeable fees in their own right.

MAP YOUR STRUCTURE

Top speakers build their speeches around a strong outline. I recommend you use the classic three-part framework.

Part One: Introduction. Your preview or introduction should grab your listeners' attention, sell your listeners on why they should listen, and provide an overview of what's to come.

Part Two: Body. The body of your speech is where you present your point of view. You make three compelling points and support them with evidence and illustrations.

Part Three: Conclusion. A strong conclusion recaps the positioning statement and key points, includes a wrap-up story, and finishes with a call for action.

PART ONE: PLAN YOUR INTRODUCTION

Dynamic speakers start strongly. You get just 30 seconds to make a powerful first impression.

A dynamic opening serves three functions. It has to:
• Grab the audience's attention. The opening must hook the audience into listening.

- Provide reasons for listening. This is where you explain to your listeners the benefits of listening—what's in it for them. This is the most critical part of persuasion.
- Describe what you'll talk about. This is where you provide a quick overview of your main points.

PART TWO: ORGANIZE THE BODY

Organize you speech around three key points. Three points are easy to remember and are psychologically persuasive. It takes approximately 10 minutes to make a point. So don't try to cover more than three points in a 30-minute speech.

Support each point with evidence. The right evidence will clinch your case. Poorly chosen evidence can destroy your presentation.

Use a mix of supports. Different people are persuaded by different types of information. Some people like statistics; others prefer anecdotes and quotes.

Use the latest information. Use illustrations, statistics, and expert testimony—the more recent the better. If your information or statistics are new and surprising, sell the fact.

PART THREE: PLAN YOUR CONCLUSION

Your conclusion is the last thing people hear. It's your last chance to get through. In a presentation, starting off badly is a setback; finishing badly often signals failure.

A strong conclusion must:
- Summarize your speech. The conclusion must recap your key points.
- Provide closure. The conclusion must end purposefully. Speeches have to "sound finished."
- Motivate the audience to respond. You must present a call to action. If your speech is informative, you may want the audience to reflect on the issues or go away and do research.

EXHIBIT 6.7

1. **Introduction**
   (10–15 percent of time)
   - **Hook:** Opening statement to grab attention
     Positioning Statement: Benefit statement selling advantages of listening
   - **Preview:** Overview of key points that support positioning statement

2. **Body**
   (80–85 percent of time)
   - **Point One:**
     Evidence/illustration
   - **Point Two:**
     Evidence/illustration
   - **Point Three:**
     Evidence/illustration

3. **Conclusion**
   (5 percent of time)
   - **Recap:** Summary of positioning statement and key points
   - **Memorable Conclusion:** Wrap-up story or statement
   - **Call for action:** Ask for the order/commitment

WOWING WITH VISUAL AIDS

If you want to increase the odds of closing a deal with a high impact presentation, you have to use visuals. Most business presenters use PowerPoint. Unfortunately, most bore their audiences by presenting text slide after text slide.

Visuals persuade
A 1986 study by the University of Minnesota and 3M found that presenters who use slides and overhead transparencies are 43 percent more persuasive than those who don't.

75 percent of what we learn comes to us visually, 13 percent through hearing and 12 percent through smell, taste, and touch.

Presenters who use computer-generated visuals come across as more professional, more interesting, and more effective.

Visuals increase retention
We quickly forget most of what we hear in a meeting where the presenter uses only words. We retain less than 10 percent of what we hear in a verbal only presentation.

However, when a speaker uses visuals as well as words, the retention rate increases dramatically, to 38 percent.

Think KISS (keep it short and simple)
With visuals, less is more. There are 33 million business presentations given every day. Most are too long and too complex.

When you create a visual, ask:
- Is it simple?
- Is it clear?
- Is it visible?

If it fails any of these three tests, redesign it.

Start with a master template
Most busy presenters don't have time or the design skills to create a visually stunning presentation.

The solution is to start with a commercially created master template created by design experts such as PresentationPro.

A visually compelling template will allow you to:
- Create visual unity
- Jazz up your presentation
- Set yourself apart from your competitors.

Stick to one idea per visual
Organize all visuals around one specific point. Keep your visuals simple and uncluttered. Ask yourself, "what is the central point I want to communicate?" Then design your visual around that point.

Each visual should have a headline or caption that clearly states what it shows. It should be simple and brief and communicate the purpose.

Search for a single visual to sell your message

Top presenters build their presentations around an organizing visual, such as a pyramid which visually communicates the central theme.

You should be able to write down the central idea or theme of your presentation. The central idea identifies the essence of your message. Think of it as a one-sentence summary of your presentation.

USING SMART PR TO GENERATE FREE PUBLICITY

Smart PR can help you create buckets of free publicity. Publicity involves supplying radio, newspapers, television stations, trade journals, newsletters, and Web sites with newsworthy, interesting information.

The purpose of the publicity is to create news and feature stories about yourself, your practice, and your services. The news can be anything from a one-line quotation in a news report to a multipage feature in a trade journal.

PRIORITIZE YOUR PUBLICITY GOALS

Successful publicity starts with setting and prioritizing your publicity goals.

Targeted publicity will:
1. Raise your practice profile within your business community
2. Enhance your image with your various publics
3. Position you as a credible expert
4. Generate sales leads.

Analyze your audience

Before you create any publicity, you must analyze your audience. As a publicist you first have to convince journalists to publicize your story. Then you need to have strong enough hooks in your story, approach, or angle to entice readers or viewers to enquire about your services.

Select your media

Once you have analyzed your audience you have to pick the stations, publications, or Web sites that will reach the specific audience you want.

Select your medium

Now that you have identified the media and audience, you can choose the right publicity tools. These can range from press releases to videos.

The news release

The news release forms the basis of most successful publicity campaigns. "If you master how to write it, where to send it and whom to send it to, you should be able to get more than 50 percent of your releases placed," says Reece Franklin, the author of *The Consultant's Guide to Publicity*.[11]

To write your news release, use the five Ws and H formula.

THE FIVE Ws AND H FORMULA

The five Ws and H are who, what, where, when, why and how. If you check the news pages of any newspaper or listen to a news broadcast, you'll notice that almost every story answers these six key questions: What happened; Where it took place; Why it occurred; When, to Whom; and How.

Once you have outlined your basic facts, you need to add the sizzle and excitement that makes journalists want to publish your material or cover your event. Look for a peg or an unusual idea to hang your story on.

FIND AN ANGLE

Successful publicists are experts at finding the right angle. According to David Yale and Andrew Carothers, authors of *The Publicity Handbook,* "the right angle, or newspeg, is the slant that makes a story interesting. With the right angle, you can transform a situation that's not in the least newsworthy into frontpage coverage."[12]

For example, if you are launching a new service, you need to answer questions such as:

- What is new or different about your service?
- How does it compare with what is out in the market now?
- What research was involved in developing it?
- How will it benefit buyers? Will it save them time or money? Will it lower risks? Will it increase opportunities?
- Who is currently using it?
- What has been the impact on the people using it?

The press release on page 149 reveals what you can achieve with imagination. Freelance copyrighter Bob Bly sent this press release to sixty U.S. advertising, public relations, and marketing publications. The results: eighteen stories plus 2,000 requests for the booklet. Bly's news release also generated additional sales for his books and marketing, and picked up several consulting assignments.

How to Write a News Release

Here are some practical tips:
1. Type the release on your letterhead.
2. Keep it brief. If you can, limit it to one page; two pages maximum.
3. Use wide margins both left and right and double spacing to make it easy to edit.
4. Date your release clearly. And put your contact name, phone number, fax, and e-mail address at the top.

5. Write simply and concisely. Use short words, short sentences, short paragraphs. Use rigorous active verbs and strive for fluency.

6. Provide a punchy informative headline. If your headline doesn't immediately say that your release has news worth reading, it won't get read.

7. Make sure the lead paragraph contains all the key information that makes your release newsworthy. Organize your copy in inverted pyramid form. The inverted pyramid format requires you to put the most important information first. Each subsequent paragraph contains less important information until the last paragraph, which contains the least significant information.

How to Get the Most Out of Your News Release

U.S.–based David Gumpert, who runs his own public relations/marketing communication business and specializes in services to professional service providers, offers these three tips to improve your chances of receiving coverage for your press release:

Consider offering several variations of a release. If you want to address different groups of media, you will probably need to create two or three different versions of the same news release.

Don't forget the local media. The local media likes to publicize local personalities.

Add photographs and graphics where appropriate. Newspapers and magazines like to use photographs and charts to break up print and make the news page more interesting.[13]

EXHIBIT 6.8

Sample press
release

FROM: Bob Bly, 174 Holland Avenue, New Milford, NJ 07646

CONTACT: Bob Bly 201-599-2277

For immediate release

Free Booklet Reveals 31 Ways to Get More Inquiries from Your Ads

New Milford, NJ—A new booklet, published by independent copywriter and advertising consultant Robert W. Bly, reveals 31 strategies for creating ads that generate more inquiries, leads, sales, and profits for advertisers.

The booklet, "31 ways to get more inquiries from your ads," is available free of charge to business executives, entrepreneurs, advertising professionals, and students.

Bly said he originally wrote the booklet for companies and ad agencies that need to see more of a bottom-line return from advertising campaigns originally designed purely to build "image" and awareness.

"There's no reason an image campaign can't also generate leads as well as awareness," says Bly. "High-quality inquiries mean more sales and profits.

And they also provide a way of measuring response. The booklet presents 31 ways to increase any ad's pulling power without destroying the basic concept or interfering with communication of the key message."

Some of the inquiry-producing techniques presented in the booklet include:

Offer free information—a booklet, brochure, catalog, price list, order form— in every ad you write.

Give your literature piece a title that implies value. "Product guide sounds better than *catalog,*" notes Bly. "*Planning kit* implies greater value than *sales brochure.*"

For a full-page ad, use a coupon. According to Bly, "This will increase response 25 to 100 percent."

Make the coupon large enough so that there is plenty of room for prospects to write their name and address. "Tiny coupons drive people crazy," notes Bly.

In a fractional ad, put a heavy dashed border around the ad. "This creates a coupon-like appearance, which in turn stimulates response," explains Bly.

Offer something FREE—such as a free product sample, free report, free video or audio cassette, free analysis, free consultation, free estimate, free seminar, free demonstration, or free trial.

Says Bly: "By modifying existing ads using the techniques outlined in this booklet, advertisers can increase response to their ads 20 to 100 percent— without destroying the basic concept and theme of these campaigns."

To receive a free copy of "31 ways to get more inquiries from your ads," send a self-addressed stamped #10 envelope to: Advertising Inquiries, 174 Holland Avenue, New Milford, NJ 07646.

Bob Bly is a freelance copywriter specializing in business-to-business and direct response advertising and the author of sixteen books, including *The Copywriter's Handbook* (Holt).

Here is an actual news release written in the style we recommend.

EXHIBIT 6.9

Sample news release

FOR IMMEDIATE RELEASE   CONTACT: Paul Franklin 714-555-686

Small Business Workshop:

Low Risk—High Profits: How Streetsmart Entrepreneurs Make Money

It's a myth that successful entrepreneurs have to take on huge risks to make money. "The most successful entrepreneurs we work with know how to minimize it—and still make stunning profits," says Paul Franklin.

Paul Franklin is conducting a series of workshops in the Southern California area on how to grow your business with minimal risk. The workshops show participants (1) how to spot, (2) manage, and (3) reduce risk while still growing their business.

The workshops are targeted at aspiring entrepreneurs and current business owners.

Paul Franklin is managing partner of xx, an accountancy firm that works mostly with small and medium-sized independent businesses.

PHOTOGRAPH ENCLOSED

Here is a model template you can use as a guide.

EXHIBIT 6.10

News release template

(On firm's stationery)

FOR IMMEDIATE RELEASE   CONTACT: Name and telephone

Date:

One- or two-line headline that summarizes key message.

Location of the firm and date.

The *lead paragraph* should contain the material that makes the news release newsworthy.

Second paragraph: Expands on the first paragraph and elaborates on the purpose of the press release.

Third paragraph: Further details with additional quote.

Fourth paragraph: Background information on firm.

BECOMING AN EXPERT NEWS SOURCE

One of the best ways to gain free publicity is to become a news source for a reporter. Few professionals appreciate how easy it is to become a news source and find yourself quoted in the business pages and being read by executives in companies you want to work with.

Reporters find it surprisingly hard to locate professionals who can generate quotable lines to add insight to a breaking story.

Your credibility as an expert source can come from:

- Your activity as an office holder in a local professional association
- Speeches or educational programs you run for clients or professional groups
- Articles or books you've written
- Your participation in newsworthy events such as noteworthy trials.

Learn How the Media Works

Larry Bodine, the operator of lawmarketing.com, says a top news source has to understand how the media works. According to Bodine:

- A source is someone who always has a quick and catchy quote he can use.
- A source is someone who calls the reporter back within the hour.
- A source is someone who, if he doesn't have the answer, will do some checking and at least get back to the reporter with something.
- A source is someone who calls from time to time with little tips and an occasional story idea.[14]

How to Become an Expert Source

The easiest way to become an expert source is to call a reporter with a suggestion for a story idea.

Before you telephone, read a selection of her stories and figure out how your expertise fits in. Remember, reporters are looking for pithy, fresh, insightful sound bites that can be tied to a current news story.

The best way to establish your credibility and professionalism with a reporter is to initially suggest a story idea that does not promote you or your firm.

"There are three important rules of dealing with the press that every professional should know," says Bodine.

"Rule One: always return reporters' calls." Reporters quickly give up on erratic communicators.

"Rule Two: call back within the hour, and within the same day in any event."

"Rule Three: give the reporter something he can use." Never say no, I can't help you. Tell her you'll do some checking and you'll call her back.

AVOID MEDIA DEATH

Reporters have pet hates. Commit any of these, and you may suffer what Larry Bodine calls "media death"—which means you'll never appear in the publication again.

Pet Hate One: Ask to review the story before publication.

Pet Hate Two: Calling back after you've made a quote, asking for changes or retraction.

Pet Hate Three: Causing a reporter to miss a deadline.

Pet Hate Four: Getting angry or belligerent.

Pet Hate Five: Saying "no comment" to a question without giving a reason why you can't respond (such as client confidentiality).

Pet Hate Six: Sources who don't understand the difference between "on the record," "off the record," and "not for attribution."

A reporter will always assume that anything you say is "on the record" unless you indicate otherwise in advance. Few reporters feel any obligation to honor an after-the-fact request to treat what you've just said as an "off-the-record" or "not-for-attribution" comment.

"Off the record" means that you cannot be quoted, and nothing you can say can be used directly. "Not for attribution" means you can be quoted as an expert, but it cannot be attributed to you.

WRITING INFLUENTIAL ARTICLES

Virtually all clients look for expertise when they hire professionals. One of the best ways to raise your expertise in your client's eyes and promote your practice is to write articles for influential trade journals, magazines, and newspapers.

THE BENEFITS OF WRITING ARTICLES

One article can generate dozens of leads. Robert Bly, an expert on copywriting and marketing consulting services, says that placing features with appropriate trade, consumer, or business magazines is one of the most powerful and effective marketing techniques for professionals because:

- You can get one, two, or more pages devoted to your product or service without paying for the space. (A paid ad of that length could run $3,000 to $20,000 or more.)
- Your message has far more credibility as "editorial material" than as a sponsored advertisement.
- The publication of the article results in prestige for the author and recognition of the company.
- Reprints make excellent, low-cost sales literature.[15]

One article alone can generate dozens of leads for your professional practice.

THE ODDS OF GETTING PUBLISHED ARE HIGH

Most professionals seem reluctant to write bylined articles for fear of rejection. Yet the chances of getting published have never been greater—if you know how.

Magazines are looking for feature articles. There are more than 6,000 magazines and trade journals in the U.S. alone, and the market is becoming more specialized. Pressures on staffing and profits mean publications are increasingly looking for articles written by outsiders. Not surprisingly, magazine editors love articles they don't have to pay for.

Most professionals don't charge for their articles because the writing fees pale when compared to the fees and engagements that can be triggered by the publication of an article.

Magazine editors are also increasingly discovering that articles written by real experts rather than freelancers carry more weight with their readers.

Nevertheless, most editors still have reservations about articles written by service professionals. Most articles written by professionals are "too technical, detailed, poorly written and just plain boring."

Your prime task is to convince the editor that you are different. And the best way to do that is to write a compelling article ready for printing.

Practical Guidelines on How to Get Published

SELECT YOUR TOPIC

Select one, two, or three subjects that you have personal, first-hand knowledge of and feel comfortable writing about. You may even find that an article you wrote for a practice newsletter can be turned into a feature article. "Ideally these should incorporate some trend rather than be generic," says David E. Gumpert. An article titled "Three New Criteria to Impress Bankers—And Get the Money You Need" will appeal more than simply "How to Get a Bank Loan."[16]

Never forget that editors are trying to entertain and intrigue as well as keep their readers up to date.

TARGET POTENTIAL PUBLICATIONS

Ask, whom do I want to read my article? What do my ideal prospects read? This will help you identify the magazines and journals to write for.

REVIEW EACH POTENTIAL PUBLICATION

Go through back copies and ask:
- Do they use outside contributors?
- What are the credentials of the outside contributors?
- What types of articles do they prefer?
- Do they have regular columnists?
- How long are the articles?

Remember, always familiarize yourself with a publication before you approach an editor.

CALL OR WRITE TO THE EDITOR

Now is the time to test your idea on the editor. I recommend you telephone. But when you do, make sure you can describe your proposal in 30 seconds or less. If the editor likes your proposal, then she will probably suggest you send in a brief outline. Do this and then follow up a few days later with a phone call.

SUBMIT A PROPOSAL

Some editors want to look at a completed article. Others will respond to your call by asking for an outline or detailed proposal.

Remember that a proposal is not a full article. As an outline it should describe the theme of the article and set out in bullet form the main points. Include lists of the case studies you want to use and add in sample graphs or diagrams. And keep the proposal to two pages or less.

SUBMIT YOUR ARTICLE ON TIME

Deadlines are critical for editors, so make sure you meet the prescribed deadline. Few editors will forgive you for delivering late copy.

BE PREPARED TO FINE-TUNE YOUR ARTICLE

Expect your editors to suggest changes. They know what their readers want to read. Editors also like to make articles fit in with the "look and feel" of their publication. So listen hard and be flexible. Writers who work well with editors often find they get further invitations for articles.

Here is a list of the common types of articles business publications look for. Use the list to spark ideas and angles for possible articles.

EXHIBIT 6.11

Sample listing of common types of business articles

- List of good and bad things (e.g., Ten Ways to Market on the Internet)
- Trends and directions (e.g., How Computers Will Change Quality Management)
- Best practices (e.g., Growing Use of Benchmarking in HR Programs)
- Studies and surveys (e.g., Supply Chain Management in 100 Firms)
- Advice and tips (e.g., Getting the Most from the Use of Coupons)
- Case studies (e.g., Corporate Renewal at Xerox)
- Techniques (e.g., Using Run Charts to Communicate Process Problems)
- Interview (e.g., Jack Welch Reveals His Secrets of Success)
- Issues (e.g., The Growing Problem of Year 2000 in American Corporations)
- Points of view (e.g., Why the Internet Is Now Safe to Use)
- Advocacy (e.g., How the ASTD Helps Trainers Perform Well)
- Catalog-like (e.g., Ten Software Tools to Support Statistical Process Control)
- Product descriptions (e.g., SAP and How Companies Use It)

James W. Cortada, Publishing Intellectual Capital (Prentice Hall PTR, 1999), p. 62.

Recycle Your Published Articles

Professional freelancers know how to recycle, i.e., print the same core article in several publications and collect a fee from each.

Recycling allows professionals to maximize their potential audience. The key to recycling, says Robert Bly, is to make sure that when you initially place the article, you license the publication for "one-time" publication rights (known as first rights) only. You, the author, keep all other rights. This means you don't have to ask for permission to use your own work in other publications.

REPRINT AND DISTRIBUTE YOUR ARTICLES

Finally, don't forget to distribute copies of your articles to current, past, and potential clients. Follow Robert Bly's advice and "Include the reprints in your literature package or press kit, leave them in the reception area or lobby, hand them out at conferences and speaking engagements, and enclose them in your direct mail."[17]

CREATE A WRITTEN PUBLICITY STRATEGY

To achieve your publicity goals, you need to write down your goals and spell out precisely how you are going to achieve them. Exhibit 6.12 is a sample draft of a publicity strategy plan.

THE POWER OF DIRECT MAIL

Direct mail is one of the most powerful tools available to increase the effectiveness of your prospecting. Professional services marketing pioneer Bruce Marcus says direct mail is the "most universally effective of all professional service marketing tools."[18]

THE IDEAL LEAD GENERATION TOOL

The best use of direct mail is to generate qualified leads. Few promotion methods can equal direct mail's effectiveness for lead generation.

EXHIBIT 6.12

Model publicity strategy plan

Publicity Goals	Actions
1. Position myself as expert in specialized area.	• Place targeted stories on practice in local and regional media • Write regular column for trade journal • Teach course to M.B.A. program.
2. Become news source when media looks for "expert" commentary in my area.	• Stay in contact with key reporters /editors • Develop ideas for new stories to pass on to reporters.
3. Generate high quality sales leads.	• Give speeches on area of expertise to client or industry sector conferences • Give seminars and workshops on area of expertise • Deliver small in-house seminars.

Direct mail is also a useful *supplementary* tool for:
• Building relationships with occasion or seasonal messages
• Encouraging loyalty and sales with newsletters
• Encouraging referrals
• Encouraging lapsed clients to reconsider your service
• Seeking client feedback
• Informing clients about new services.

However, don't expect direct mail to work as a stand-alone sales tool. Remember, letters don't sell professional services—people do.

THE 60-15-15-10 RULE

Keep in mind the 60-15-15-10 rule when you create your direct mail.

60 percent of successful mail depends on identifying and reaching the right people. The best offer sent to the wrong audience is doomed to failure.

15 percent of successful mail depends on the appeal and attractiveness of your offer.

15 percent of successful mail depends on timing.

10 percent of a successful result depends on the creative content of your mailing. So, don't get too obsessed with the creativity and writing.

Start by identifying **who** first, **what** second, and **when** third. Finally, consider creativity and writing.

Here are the three initial questions you must start with:
1. Whom do we want to target?
2. What offer should we make?
3. When should we do it?[19]

FINDING AND USING GOOD MAILING LISTS

It can be profitable to rent a list from a list broker—so long as the list is current and precisely meets your target destination.

Since the prospects on a commercially acquired list don't know you, it pays to adopt a less familiar tone in your writing than when you direct mail your own database.

For this reason, you may need to significantly modify letters you have successfully sent to your database and plan to resend to a commercially acquired list.

TEST, TEST, TEST

Direct mail is unique in that you can test different approaches and ideas. What works on a small sample is likely to work equally well on a large one.

How to Write Letters that Persuade

A persuasive letter is an essential part of a successful direct mail package. Author and direct marketing consultant Dick Hodgson says, "it is crucial to keep in mind the five musts" of good direct mail writing:

- Is it clear?
- Is it interesting?
- Is it concise?
- Is it believable?
- Is it friendly?[20]

THE AIDA FORMULA

Direct mail is full of formulas designed to provide guidelines for copy writers.

The most popular by far is AIDA.

A Attract the reader's **attention**

I Arouse the reader's **interest** in the offer

D Stimulate the reader's **desire** to take action

A Ask the reader to take the **action** requested.

BOB STONE'S SEVEN-STEP FORMULA

I've found out of all the formulas, Professor Bob Stone's is the most useful:

1. Promise a benefit in your headline or first paragraph—*your most important benefit*.
2. Immediately enlarge your most important benefit.
3. Tell the reader *specifically* what he or she is going to get.
4. Back up your statements with *proof* and *endorsements*.
5. Tell the reader what might be lost if he or she doesn't act.
6. Rephrase your prominent benefits in your closing.
7. Incite action—*now*.[21]

Here is a sample lead-generating letter written by Bob Bly.[22]

Dear Marketing Professional

"It's hard to find a copywriter who can handle industrial and high-tech accounts," a prospect told me over the phone today. "Especially for brochures, direct mail, and other long-copy assignments."

Do you have that same problem?

If so, please complete and mail the enclosed reply card, and I'll send you a free information kit describing a service that can help.

As a freelance copywriter specializing in business-to-business marketing, I've written hundreds of successful ads, sales letters, direct mail packages, brochures, data sheets, annual reports, feature articles, press releases, newsletters, and audio-visual scripts for clients all over the country.

But my information kit will give you the full story.

You'll receive a comprehensive "WELCOME" letter that tells all about my copywriting service—who I work for, what I can do for you, how we can work together.

You'll also get my client list (I've written copy for more than 100 corporations and agencies); client testimonials; biographical background; samples of work I've done in your field; a fee schedule listing of what I charge for ads, brochures, and other assignments; helpful article reprints on copywriting and advertising; even an order form you can use to put me to work for you.

Whether you have an immediate project, a future need, or are just curious, I urge you to send for this information kit. It's free—there's no obligation—and you'll like having a proven copywriting resource on file—someone you can call on whenever you need him.

From experience, I've learned that the best time to evaluate a copywriter and take a look at his work is before you need him, not when a project deadline comes crashing around the corner. You want to feel comfortable about a writer and his capabilities in advance, so when a project does come up, you know who to call.

Why not mail back the reply card TODAY, while it is still handy? I'll rush your free information kit as soon as I hear from you.

Regards
Bob Bly

P.S. Need an immediate quote on a copywriting project? Call me at 201-385-1220. There is no charge for a cost estimate. And no obligation to buy.

EXHIBIT 6.14

The sixteen most persuasive words

Here is a list of the 16 most persuasive words used in direct mail. Wherever you can, incorporate these in your letters.

you/your	money
guarantee	love
easy	benefit
results	proven
fun	new
now	health
save	free
how to	safe

E-MAIL MARKETING THAT SELLS

The e-mail channel is emerging as one of the most profitable and economical ways to promote professional services. E-mail marketing is now a billion dollar industry.

According to a 2000 Jupiter Communications Report, [23] companies are using e-mail marketing to:

- Deepen the relationship with the customer—61 percent
- Acquire new customers—46 percent
- Cross-sell—29 percent
- Up-sell—29 percent
- Shorten the purchase cycle—18 percent
- Other—11 percent

Why is e-mail marketing exploding in popularity? Yes Mail's Scott Stephen says: "E-mail has proven itself to be a fast and efficient marketing vehicle. It is more responsive than other forms of direct marketing—online or off. It is more cost effective than other direct marketing media. E-mail is easily integrated into an overall marketing plan."

E-MAIL NOW COMES IN MULTIPLE FORMATS

Advances in technology have also turned e-mail from a plain vanilla text medium into a multimedia offering, which incorporates color, text, page formatting, graphics, and audio and video. The result is increasing response rates.

ALWAYS ASK FOR PERMISSION

In his book *Permission Marketing,* Seth Godin put forward the then radical notion of asking prospects or customers for permission before attempting to communicate with them.[24]

No reputable professional firm wants to be branded a spammer, so whether you are renting a list or using your firm's list for your mailing, make sure you have the recipients' permission to mail to them.

How to Run a Successful E-mail Marketing Campaign

Military style planning is the basis of successful e-mail campaigns. Here are some general guidelines to keep you on track.[25]

Step 1: Establish your campaign goals
Start by listing the specific, measurable and trackable goals you plan to achieve. For example:
- Calculate the specific number of leads you want to generate
- Calculate the number of prospects you want to sign up for your newsletter.

Step 2: Segment your market
Clearly identify the target group of prospects you want to influence. Ask, exactly what groups do we want to communicate with?

Step 3: Specify your call(s) to action
Ask, precisely what do you want those who receive your e-mail to do? Do you want the recipient to:

- Download a white paper
- Attend a seminar
- Respond to an invitation
- Sign up for a survey
- Visit a specific Web page.

Step 4: Decide on your message format

It is possible to create your message in a variety of formats. These include text, HTML, and RichMedia formats. Each format has different pros and cons. Review each one.

Step 5: Write and design your content

To persuade your message must be personalized, easy to read, relevant, and benefit orientated. Your message should also include your privacy policy and an unsubscribe mechanism.

Step 6: Estimate the number of mailings

Most campaigns consist of simple mailings, but campaigns often work better when they consist of a number of related messages spaced over time. These need to be planned.

Step 7: Measure your responses

There are a variety of ways to measure e-mail campaign response rates. There are several outsourcers who have the software to measure what you need. Choose the one that best suits your needs.

Step 8: Organize your internal resources to handle responses

Make sure you have the resources in place to quickly respond if your campaign is as successful as you hoped. Prospects are quickly turned off by slow response times to e-mail campaigns.

Step 9: Plan for unsubscribing and bounces

Make it as easy as possible for a recipient to unsubscribe.

Two to 20% of your messages will come back as "bounced messages." Bounced messages come in two forms:
1. hard (c-mail address doesn't exist)
2. soft (their server is down or their mailbox is full).

Hard bounces have to be deleted. Soft bounces have to be resent.

Step 10: Test your message on a variety of platforms and systems
Test that your message can be read by a variety of browsers and clients outside your network.

Professional firms have generally been cautious in their use of e-mail marketing. If you have doubts about its effectiveness I suggest you start building up your skills by using e-mail to alert your clients about changes in your industry. Many law firms use their Web sites to notify clients of impending changes in the law.

The more adventurous package their analysis into branded style HTML e-mails and send them directly to their clients' desktops.

When Benesch, Friedlander, Coplan and Asonoff, LLP, a 130-attorney Ohio firm, used branded HTML e-mail to alert its clients about provisions in the impending Sarbanes-Oxley Act, 66 percent of clients opened the e-mail and 38 percent clicked onto a Web link to learn more.

By using a tracking mechanism provided by eLawMarketing, which ran the campaign, Benesch was also able to identify which clients clicked the "full analysis" link, telling them which clients would be most receptive to additional followup after the campaign.

MARKETING WITH CLIENT NEWSLETTERS

Client newsletters provide one of the best vehicles for reaching important markets and decision makers. Newsletters can be tremendously effective when they deliver insightful, up-to-date information. But too often, writes Mark Butler, a legal firm consultant with Altman Weil, newsletters damage practice reputations by "trying to pass off stale information and self-promotion as news."

There are two types of newsletters: subscription newsletters and promotional newsletters.

Subscription newsletters, which typically charge an annual fee, provide hard news or "need to know" information.

Promotional newsletters are delivered free by a firm to its clients, prospective clients, and referral sources.

The purpose of a promotional newsletter is to:

- Build name and brand recognition
- Demonstrate the firm's areas of expertise by providing practical advice
- Establish a reputation for insightful commentary and analysis
- Show you can explain difficult, complex technical concepts in easy-to-follow language.

Newsletters that really do inform typically have a 400 to 700 percent higher readership than standard brochures and direct mail.

However, newsletters are time consuming. The planning, set-up time, the article writing coordination, text input, editing, and proofreading are such that many small and mid-sized firms find it's more economical to outsource their newsletter(s) to a public relations firm or newsletter company.

How to Promote Your Newsletter

Award winning U.S. newsletter consultant David Freedman says there are a dozen ways to ensure your newsletter gets read, passed around, and quoted.[26]

1. **Keep the marketing objective narrow.** One newsletter can accomplish one marketing objective, no more.
2. **Make sure the editor understands the marketing objective** and writes and edits with that in mind.
3. **Pretend it's a subscription newsletter.** This will make your writing tighter, more disciplined, and more insightful.
4. **Keep the news about your firm to a minimum.** Let the articles and advice do the selling.

5. **Narrow down the topics and cover them in depth.** Go for depth rather than breadth. Short, shallow, superficial articles will quickly destroy your credibility.
6. **Be specific.** Provide lots of definitions, examples, and anecdotes; specifics persuade, while broad generalities create frustration.
7. **Stay in touch with your readers and respond to their changing needs.** Regularly survey your readers so they can tell you what they need.
8. **Give the reader many points of entry.** As well as full-length features, add short features, news briefs, regular columns, and sidebars. Give every item a punchy heading.
9. **Include a response mechanism.** For readers who want additional information, offer to fax, e-mail, or mail free material the firm has prepared in advance.
10. **Be punctilious.** Proofread, proofread, proofread. Good grammar, punctuation, and style show you demand high standards.
11. **No gratuitous graphics.** Above all, avoid clip art.
12. **Send the newsletter to "thought leaders."** Circulate your newsletter to anyone who influences your prime audience. Don't forget trade associations, libraries, reporters, and regulatory agencies.

MOVING TO E-MAIL NEWSLETTERS

Newsletters have taken on a new life with the introduction of e-mail. Mark Pruner, the president of Web Counsel, LLC (http.webcounsel.com), a marketer who consults to U.S. law firms, says, "An e-mailed newsletter can be the most cost-effective marketing that a law firm does."[27] This comment can be extended to virtually all types of professional firms.

ADVANTAGES OVER TRADITIONAL NEWSLETTERS

An e-mail newsletter has significant advantages over its traditional counterpart. E-mail newsletters are much cheaper to distribute.

With an e-mail newsletter, one click and out it goes to your entire mailing list. An e-mail newsletter send-out costs a fraction of a print campaign.

An e-mail newsletter has almost zero marginal cost. Each additional subscriber can be added for minimal cost. Readers can store e-mail newsletters easily or, even better, forward it on to others. Because they are sent via the Internet, e-mail newsletters can be hyperlinked to additional sources on the Internet. It's much easier to track the results of e-mail newsletters than traditional newsletters.

ASCI, HTML, OR VISUAL MAIL

Lots of firms still send plain text or ASCI text mail. With older computers, ASCI or text e-mail is much quicker to download than HTML enhanced mail. However, this is becoming much less of a problem as clients upgrade their machines.

With an HTML enhanced e-mail you can format your newsletter to look much the same as any printed newsletter. The addition of different fonts, graphics, and color has a huge impact on readability and results. In measured sales tests HTML e-mail performs at least twice as well (measured by sales and response rates) as plain text e-mail.

The latest type of e-mail is visual mail. Visual mail allows you to add motion and interaction to the e-mail. Animation sound and video can be embedded in the e-mail, as well as graphics. This type of delivery is called *rich media*.

Once you add lots of graphics you increase the size of files enormously. To overcome this problem, proprietary compression programs such as EmailPresenter (www.presentationpro.com) enable large visual e-mail presentations to be "shrunk" by 75 percent or more.

Writing Your Electronic Newsletter

Writing to be read on a computer screen demands different techniques. The four keys, says Rachel McAlpine, the author of *Web Word Wizardry*, are:

- "Write concisely
- Write objectively
- Use a readable design
- Write to be scanned." [28]

WRITE CONCISELY

Omit needless words. Cut the number of words you would use in your normal paper newsletter by 50 percent. Research shows reading from a computer screen is about 25 percent slower.

WRITE OBJECTIVELY

Hype and hyperbole don't sell. Stick to the facts and let the quality of your professional insights and comments do the selling.

USE A READABLE DESIGN

Keep the design simple and clean. Make it look and feel like a traditional newsletter.

Use a dark text on a pale background. Black text on a white background is the most readable.

Use short words, short sentences, and short paragraphs.
- Limit your line length to 12 words.
- Keep your average sentence length down to 12 words or less.
- Limit your paragraphs to four lines or less.

Use lots of white space. Leave extra white space at the top of the screen. Use wide margins and lots of subheadings and pull quotes to create visual relief.

Choose easy-to-read fonts. For legibility, it is hard to go past Times Roman and Helvetica. Stay away from fancy fonts and, above all, avoid italics. Italics can't be read on many screens.

Use 11- or 12-point font size. For your body text, use a font size of 11 to 12 points. Most readers find this comfortable to read.

Use lower case. Keep the use of capitals to an absolute minimum. Solid capitals are very difficult to read. Words in lower case are much easier to read.

WRITE TO BE SCANNED

- *Use lots of headings.* Make your headings clear, informative, and to the point. Good headings and subheadings quickly guide you through a newsletter and make a terrific difference! Leave more space above a heading than below it, and make subheadings clearly subordinate to your main headings.

- *Use explanatory headings.* A longer descriptive heading works better than one that is too terse and uninformative.

- *Use lots of bulleted lists.* Bullets are a breeze to scan. Three to five items in a list is ideal.

Tracking Results

When it comes to measuring results, e-mail newsletters are superior to traditional newsletters.

If you place a unique graphic in a newsletter, all you have to do is count the number of times the graphic has been loaded, and, presto, you have a measure of the number of times the newsletter has been viewed.

Each time a subscriber downloads an image, your Web site records the domain that requested the file.

The actual timing of the downloads tells you when your newsletter is being downloaded and read. Is it at work, at home, during the week, or on the weekends? Once you have this type of information, you can further refine your approach.

SEEK FEEDBACK

Each newsletter should have an e-mail link so the reader can contact you. Ask for comments. The best feedback comes from specific questions and surveys.

FAILURE TO FOLLOW THROUGH

Mark Pruner says, "By far the biggest failure of firms using e-mail marketing is a failure to effectively follow-up leads. To do all the work involved and then fail to follow-up leads will ultimately kill any marketing program," according to Mark Pruner. "Each firm," says Pruner, "should designate someone to respond immediately and acknowledge receipt."[29]

Pruner has found most attorneys (the clients he mainly serves) are too busy to compose appropriate replies, so someone else has to take responsibility.

Here is a model reply composed by Mark Pruner.

Dear Mr. Smith

We have received your e-mail inquiring about the new HIPPA regulations. I have spoken with Ms. Johnson, our HIPPA expert, and she will contact you tomorrow morning. Would either 9:30 or 11:45AM be convenient for you?

In the meantime she thought you might be interested in this article that she wrote entitled "The Ten Things that Every General Counsel Needs to Know About the New Health Privacy Regulations." You can see the article on our website at [URL] and you can see Ms. Johnson's bio at [URL].

Please let me know what time would be most convenient. If you have any questions, please feel free to call me at 203-969-7900.

This is the type of reply that makes a client want to work with you.

When you've reached this stage, e-mail marketing has achieved all it can. It's now time for a face-to-face meeting.

Growing Your Subscription List

It's tempting once you discover the power of e-mail newsletters to turbo charge your efforts by buying lists of commercial e-mail addresses. Don't, even if the seller promises you it is a double opt-in list. You'll damage your firm's credibility.

However, Mark Pruner does recommend working with a related organization that already has an e-mail newsletter, "like a trade association and putting information in about your newsletter."[30] This is the way to expand your mailing list.

Because of its power and cost effectiveness, every professional firm should consider implementing an e-mail newsletter marketing program.

ADVERTISING FOR RESULTS

Many professional service firms aren't even convinced that half the money they spend on advertising can be justified. Nonetheless, there has been a dramatic upsurge in advertising among professional service firms in recent years. Accenture spent $175 million rebranding itself after it broke away from Andersen. Ernst & Young spent nearly $100 million on advertising in 2000. KPMG spent $60 million. Even law firms like Boston's Hale and Dorr are running ads.

The Law Marketing Association (LMA) 2001 study on law firm marketing budgets revealed advertising was the fifth largest item of marketing expenditure—after marketing department compensation (1), attorney client meals and entertainment (2), tickets (3) and charitable and civic event sponsorships (4).

The largest firm surveyed spent $2,200,000 on advertising; the median firm spent $67,210; while some firms spent nothing. The median expenditure of $67,210 on advertising compared to a median expenditure of $161,000 on client meals and entertainment.[31]

Should you then advertise? The answer is, it depends. If your rainmaking referral and PR programs aren't pulling enough targeted clients, you probably need to advertise. "Advertising can reach more people cheaper (per exposure) and faster than personal contact" say marketing professors Philip Kotler, Thomas Hayes, and Paul Bloom.[32]

The nature of the message you want to sell is important. Complicated messages don't easily lend themselves to advertising. "But for organizations selling relatively uncomplicated services to markets accustomed to seeing the advertising of competitors— such as personal injury law—advertising may be a necessity." [33]

IMAGE VS. RESPONSE ADVERTISING

Ads can be split into two groups: image advertisements and response advertisements.

Image advertisements communicate a general feeling about your firm. They don't call for a specific response, such as a phone call. Their task is to *gradually shift perceptions*. Image advertising is therefore often synchronized with other marketing efforts, like publicity.

Response advertisements sell a specific message and call for a specific action. The value of image advertising is much harder to measure. If you've got a limited budget, focus on response advertising.

WHERE DOES IT PAY TO ADVERTISE?

There is no ideal medium. But choosing media because they are cheap or avoiding them because they cost a lot is foolish. "A five dollar ad that gets you no business is expensive, a $1,000 ad that draws $20,000 in sales is a raving bargain," says Anthony Putnam, author of *Marketing Your Services*.[34]

YELLOW PAGES

Most professional firms find a Yellow Pages ad is an essential part of their marketing mix.

Yellow Pages ads work particularly well if:

- Clients "need you urgently." A disaster makes people reach for the Yellow Pages.
- Clients "typically need you infrequently." If you provide a service people don't use a lot, they are less likely to already have someone in mind.
- Clients "immediately associate their need with your Yellow Pages category."

"If you meet all three criteria, invest in a great Yellow Pages ad," says professional service marketing consultant Anthony O. Putnam.[35]

SPECIALIZED DIRECTORIES

Virtually every profession has one or more specialized directories, which are essentially more targeted versions of the Yellow Pages. For example, The American Society for Training and Development (ASTD) directory lists all the firms who provide training.

Should you pay to advertise in specialized directories? Yes. Alan Weiss, the author of *Million Dollar Consulting* and a clutch of other successful marketing books for consultants, has enjoyed enormous returns from his listings in industry directories such as the ASTD. If your competitors are listed in a directory, you probably need to be there as well.

Very few prospects call you and hire you as a result of a listing in a specialized directory. But prospects will request brochures or ask you to submit a proposal.

Directories represent a long-term commitment because they can be put in the marketplace for a year or more. If the number of prospects and quality of prospects generated by the listing exceeds your minimum requirements for an ad, continue to advertise in the directory. If it doesn't, drop it.

MAGAZINES

Magazines offer important advantages for professional firms. Because magazines target specific audiences, "they are a precise medium." "If your 'reach' goal is precise, the right magazine can give you 90 percent of your desired audience," says advertising consultant and author Sarah White.[36]

A continually appearing ad allows you to build your image over time, project your personality, and develop a consistent message.

The big downside with magazine advertising is cost. Compared to other print media such as newspapers, the cost of a magazine ad is high.

BUSINESS PUBLICATIONS

Business publications allow you to target vertical markets *(Paper Trade Journals* or *Graphic Arts Monthly)* by job function *(Business Marketing)* or by region *(Corporate Report Wisconsin)*.

Many readers of professional and trade publications are on the look-out for services, so they are just as likely to read an ad as an article. When you talk to prospects or clients, ask them what trade and professional journals they read and are influenced by the most.

GENERAL CIRCULATION MAGAZINES

Few professional firms find advertising in consumer magazines at all profitable, even though some mass circulation publications now offer up to 500 different regional editions.

The exceptions are where your services specifically cater to a niche represented by the magazine's audience. For example, cosmetic surgeons have found it profitable to advertise in women's consumer magazines.

NEWSPAPERS

Daily newspapers at best represent marginal value for most professional firms. The readership of a typical daily newspaper is too broad. The shelf life of a newspaper ad is also very short.

Some professional firms who sell low-value transaction services such as wills have found advertising in the "free" weekly community newspaper worthwhile.

BILLBOARDS

Outdoor advertising is an "old" media that offers a lot of advantages if you want to reach a geographically targeted market inexpensively. Outdoor advertising is surprisingly easy and cheap to create. The big limitation is message length. If the message can't be summarized in five to seven words, don't use a billboard. Billboard campaigns can be stunningly effective. They do however require imaginative execution and creative flair to work.

BROADCAST ADVERTISING: RADIO AND TV

Professional service firms have struggled to make radio and television advertising profitable.

Radio as a medium seems to cheapen professional services. Radio works through the ears and relies more than any other medium on repetition and simple memorable messages.

Television is too expensive for most professional service firms to even contemplate. You need a huge budget to make an impact. And even if you do have the budget, the brutal truth is there are many more effective ways to spend your marketing dollar.

AIDA

Remember, ads can be image based or action based. If you want to measure results, go for action.

Every action-based ad should follow the AIDA process. First you have to win the viewers or readers Attention, second you have to create Interest, third you have to create a Desire, and finally you have to ask for Action.[37] Exhibit 6.15 is a list of strong verbs to add muscle to your copy.

CREATING THE ADS

Conceiving, copyrighting, and producing an ad require expert outside help. However, it is your job to drive the strategy. You need to know what market you want to reach and what benefits you want to sell. Finally, you should have analyzed the rationale behind your choice of benefit.

EXHIBIT 6.15

Verbs that sell professional services

Align	Command	Achieve
Assure	Commit	Amplify
Boost	Compete	Announce
Design	Control	Compel
Discriminate	Develop	Convert
Foster	Differentiate	Dominate
Grow	Discover	Engineer
Improve	Distinguish	Expand
Invent	Encompass	Gain
Lever	Enhance	Mobilize
Multiply	Focus	Out distance
Out perform	Forecast	Outlast
Overcome	Influence	Pay off
Persuade	Insure	Penetrate
Predict	Integrate	Profit
Protect	Minimize	Recommend
Revitalize	Motivate	Reduce
Reward	Pinpoint	Renew
Solve	Position	Restructure
Sustain	Raise	Safeguard
Transform	Reap	Streamline
Trust	Redefine	Advise
Value	Relieve	Program

Planning for Success

To ensure success you need a media plan. Your media plan should consist of a calendar, a budget, and measurable targets you want to achieve.

Your calendar should list each media outlet where you want to place your ads. That calendar will list the magazines, billboards, and directories where you place your ads. You also need to carefully plan the timing of the ads to achieve maximum impact. The budget should be based on the amount you need to realistically achieve your targeted results.

Furthermore, you need to list the measures that will allow you to monitor the changes in attitudes or behaviors you want to achieve in quantifiable terms.[38]

STEPS

1. Identify profitable segments and niches where you can dominate.

2. Design a small group seminar program focused on the key problems your most valuable clients face.

3. Train all your professionals in presentation skills until they can present with pizzazz, flair, and impact.

4. Use the speaker evaluation template to assess all your firm's public presentations.

5. Review your key PowerPoint presentations for visual impact.

6. Have a graphics designer prepare a set of key visuals to summarize the key concepts that underpin most of your presentations.

7. Prepare a publicity strategy plan for all your key professionals based on the model publicity strategy plan.

8. Identify the areas where direct mail can make a cost-effective contribution to your marketing goals.

9. Make e-mail marketing an integral part of your marketing efforts.

10. Review the effectiveness of your current newsletters.

11. Wherever possible move from printed to e-mail newsletters.

12. Consider advertising if your referral and PR efforts are not generating enough prime prospects.

13. Develop an advertising strategy aim to precisely target your most profitable prospects.

8Rs

reacquisition · referral · regeneration · retention · rainmaking · revitalization · reputation · related · *of client relationship marketing*

TAKE THE RAINMAKING TEST

1. Do you know the psychological profile of what it takes to become a top performing seller of professional services?

   ☐ Yes   ☐ No

2. Do you know what percentage of your sales are made by the top 20 percent of your rainmakers?

   ☐ Yes   ☐ No

3. Have you trained all your professional staff in the art of consultative selling?

   ☐ Yes   ☐ No

4. Have you trained all of your staff in how to negotiate to retain margin?

   ☐ Yes   ☐ No

5. Have you trained all your professionals in presentation skills?

   ☐ Yes   ☐ No

6. Do you compile win/loss reports to measure why you win or lose competition bids?

   ☐ Yes   ☐ No

7. Do you have a structured model PowerPoint presentation to guide staff when making presentations sales pitches?

   ☐ Yes   ☐ No

CHAPTER 7

RAINMAKING

*How to sell and close
new high-margin deals*

Features

- Selecting the right rainmaker
- Measuring your sales IQ
- Selling the value-added solution
- The client-driven selling process
- Negotiating to retain margin
- Writing a winning sales proposal
- Delivering a compelling sales presentation
- The seven-step persuasion sequence
- Action steps

SELECTING THE RIGHT RAINMAKER

To win new business, especially in markets characterized by large, complex sales, you need skilled salespeople or "rainmakers." Large professional service firms have dozens of skilled rainmakers. But in a small professional service firm, it's not uncommon to find just a lead rainmaker who initiates and closes most of the large new deals.

Firms lucky enough to possess a surplus of rainmakers can grow spectacularly—especially if they are smart enough to lock the clients in with equally spectacular service.

But are top rainmakers born or made? Research suggests that the elite rainmakers who relish selling and seem to close deals effortlessly possess a cluster of psychological traits that predisposes them toward sales success.

Some of the most practical insights come from Herb Greenberg, Harold Weinstein, and Patrick Sweeney's book *How to Hire and Develop Your Next Top Performer.*[1] Greenberg, Weinstein, and Sweeney are senior executives with Caliper, a leading management consulting firm that has spent forty years developing psychological tests and tools to identify the psychological qualities of top sales performers.

A top sales person, according to Caliper, belongs to the 20 percent of sales people who sell 80 percent of all that is sold. Caliper's testing shows successful rainmakers possess five special qualities: empathy, ego-drive, service motivation, conscientiousness, and ego-strength.

QUALITY 1: EMPATHY—THE GUIDANCE SYSTEM

Caliper defines empathy as "the ability to sense the reactions of other people." It is the ability to read the body talk of any other person so you can accurately assess what he or she is thinking and listening to.

Because sales involves evasions, objections, and changing needs, salespeople have to be empathetic and flexible enough to constantly adjust their approach.

QUALITY 2: EGO-DRIVE—THE NEED TO GET A YES

Empathy by itself is not enough. Salespeople also need the motivation to use the empathy they create as a persuasion tool. Caliper labels this motivation as "ego-drive."[2]

Salespeople who possess ego-drive have a personal need to close. Successful salespeople have a psychological need to convince and to persuade to remain fulfilled and motivated. "Ego-drive is to the salesperson what fuel is to an automobile engine. In selling, ego-drive is that fuel, while empathy provides the steering."[3]

QUALITY 3: SERVICE MOTIVATION—THE NEED TO HEAR "THANK YOU"

A motivational drive to provide superior service is also critical to success in the selling of professional services. Service motivated people are driven by the need to hear "thank you, you did a good job." Service-motivated people love to be liked, and they try as hard to succeed at this as the ego-driven person does to get the prospect to say yes.

QUALITY 4: CONSCIENTIOUSNESS—THE DISCIPLINE FROM WITHIN

To succeed as a rainmaker you have to possess the discipline to remain on task and focused. Caliper has identified two forms of conscientiousness, the first "internally driven" and the second "externally driven."

Inner-driven personalities don't need sticks and carrots to motivate them. They combine high levels of "self-drive" with a high level of responsibility.

Externally driven personalities also display a high level of responsibility; however, they have to be told what to do. "Ultimately they are driven by the rules and expectation of others." Externally driven personalities have to be managed to be driven. In other words, the externally driven sales personality needs tight, ongoing management.

QUALITY 5: EGO-STRENGTH—THE KEY TO RESILIENCE

When it comes to the crunch, selling is basically a game of beating the odds of rejection. Successful salespeople have to be resilient enough to bounce back from objections and failure.

Unsuccessful salespeople punish themselves when they fail. Salespeople with ego-strength have the ability to put disappointments and rejections aside and get on with the next sale.

Hunters and Farmers

Caliper's research shows that successful salespeople can be further divided into two broad groups—"hunters" and "farmers."

"Hunters are the classically driven, highly persuasive, fast-closing salespeople. Then there are the farmers, who slowly cultivate clients, build long-lasting relationships and close less frequent, but larger sales."[4]

If you have to choose between a hunter and farmer, you should choose the person who best matches the profile of your typical sale.

Since most professional service providers earn their biggest profits from selling more value-added solutions built over time, we would strongly recommend you look for farmers.

In professional services, an aggressive ego-drive should be strongly tempered by a desire to tailor a solution that fits each client's unique needs.

If top rainmakers are indeed born, the obvious lesson would seem to be to hire and train staff who already possess the psychological traits to sell. But that's rarely possible in a professional service environment where the price requirement for recruitment has to be technical expertise.

Here are some of the ways successful firms have overcome this predicament.

1. They hire a professional rainmaker to lead the sales efforts. This super-rainmaker coordinates and mobilizes a team of the professionals. The large accounting firms have been doing this for more than a decade. The practice is even becoming more common among the larger law firms.

2. The best firms intensely train the potential rainmakers in the firm in advanced selling, negotiation, and presentation skills. The Caliper research suggests that one in four professionals possess the psychological traits to sell well. But if you want people to take on

the rainmaking for others, you need to significantly reduce the chargeable hours they are expected to bill.

3. The best firms still train everyone in the professional team in core consultative selling, presentation, and negotiation skills. The odds of success in winning a big deal dramatically increase if everyone in the team follows the same sales process and knows what to do and, just as importantly, what not to do.

   A casual but foolish remark by an untrained staff member that "you desperately need the work" to a prospect can in one short breath undermine all the efforts of your rainmakers to position your firm as a provider of premium services.

4. The best firms make sure the "nonrainmakers" are held accountable for fulfilling their quotas of referrals, presenting seminars, attending client functions, and so on. Winning new business is pushed and promoted as a team effort.

WHAT CAN A VALID PSYCHOLOGICAL TEST ACHIEVE?

If you are looking to hire specialist rainmakers, a psychological test can be worthwhile. A good psychological test can also provide insights into what marketing activities your professionals will succeed at.

Here is what you can expect a comprehensive psychological test to tell you.

- Does the individual have persuasive motivation?
- Can he or she listen effectively?
- Can he or she take rejection?
- Does the individual have service motivation?
- Is the individual assertive enough to ask for an order and tenacious enough to follow through?
- Can the individual organize his or her work and time and follow up on the work of others?
- Can he or she make decisions?
- Does the individual have the potential to grow on the job, or can he or she only be expected to perform at the entry level?

- Is he or she intensely competitive or laid back?
- Can the individual cope with detail sufficiently?
- Is the individual shrewd in judging situations, as well as people?
- Is the individual an original, innovative, creative thinker, or is he or she tradition-bound?"[5]

MEASURE YOUR SALES IQ

Selling professional services demands a high level of skill. We developed the Sales IQ test to help our professional service clients assess the face-to-face and interpersonal sales competencies of their professional staff. To sell successfully you must be able to:

- Establish your professional credibility
- Tailor your selling to meet each client's needs
- Gain entry into difficult accounts
- Take on competitors and win
- Understand buyer psychology
- Control the buying process through high-impact questioning
- Present with flair
- Gain customer commitment
- Negotiate win-win agreements.

Read the questions before you take the test. Most of the professionals who have completed the test comment that they are surprised by the sheer range and depth of interpersonal skills required to sell professional services successfully.

The smarter professionals also remark that many of the advanced interpersonal skills required to sell are essentially the same interpersonal skills you need to be a skillful accountant, lawyer, engineer, or consultant.

EXHIBIT 7.1

The Sales IQ questionnaire

The Sales IQ questionnaire is designed to help you to identify the sales skills behaviors needed to sell professional services.

Assess your Sales IQ by answering the following questions. Mark the option that best describes your performance. If your answer is "never," check Option 1. If you answer is "sometimes," check Option 3 and so on.

Option
1. Never
2. Seldom
3. Sometimes
4. Often
5. Always

When you have completed all the questions, total your scores and turn to the end to evaluate your performance.

Establishing credibility

1. I consciously establish my credentials or qualifications before I try to influence somebody.

   | 1 | 2 | 3 | 4 | 5 |

2. When persuading I offer proof of how clients have been able to trust me or my firm in the past.

   | 1 | 2 | 3 | 4 | 5 |

3. I consciously make a powerful impression in the first few minutes of any meeting.

   | 1 | 2 | 3 | 4 | 5 |

4. I consciously use body language to influence clients.

   | 1 | 2 | 3 | 4 | 5 |

5. I constantly interpret my client's body talk.

   | 1 | 2 | 3 | 4 | 5 |

6. I consciously mirror or match my client's body talk.

   | 1 | 2 | 3 | 4 | 5 |

7. I monitor what other people say for signs of deception.

   | 1 | 2 | 3 | 4 | 5 |

8. I use a low voice pitch when I want my voice to project authority.

   | 1 | 2 | 3 | 4 | 5 |

9. I vary my vocal tempo and use pauses to create interest and impact.

   | 1 | 2 | 3 | 4 | 5 |

10. When speaking I talk positively, assertively, and decisively.

   | 1 | 2 | 3 | 4 | 5 |

11. I analyze the words and behavior of the client, to assess the type of information that will persuade them.

| 1 | 2 | 3 | 4 | 5 |

12. I analyze the words and behavior of the clients I want to influence, to assess the way they prefer to make decisions.

| 1 | 2 | 3 | 4 | 5 |

Uncovering and developing needs

13. Before I begin interviewing clients I gather lots of background information.

| 1 | 2 | 3 | 4 | 5 |

14. I always plan out my questions on paper before I interview a client.

| 1 | 2 | 3 | 4 | 5 |

15. When I first meet a decision maker, I ask lots of historical or background questions.

| 1 | 2 | 3 | 4 | 5 |

16. I consciously use planned questioning sequences to get the clients to reveal their problems.

| 1 | 2 | 3 | 4 | 5 |

17. Once I've pinned down a client's problem, I use "disturbing" questions to get the client to appreciate the size and complexity of the problem.

| 1 | 2 | 3 | 4 | 5 |

18. I actively listen and use paraphrasing to continually reflect the content and feelings of my clients.

| 1 | 2 | 3 | 4 | 5 |

19. I question the clients to reveal their decision criteria and what weight they assign to each criteria.

| 1 | 2 | 3 | 4 | 5 |

Proposing value-added solutions

20. I regularly gather intelligence on the strengths and weaknesses of my competitors.

| 1 | 2 | 3 | 4 | 5 |

21. For each proposal I analyze how my firm's strengths and weaknesses compare to our likely competitors.

| 1 | 2 | 3 | 4 | 5 |

22. When presenting a proposal I demonstrate and confirm how the proposal meets the client's decision criteria.

| 1 | 2 | 3 | 4 | 5 |

23. I consciously plan my presentation strategy to expose and outflank actual or potential competitors.

    | 1 | 2 | 3 | 4 | 5 |

24. I don't offer a solution until I'm in a position to prove that the solution has been specifically tailored to meet the precise needs of the client.

    | 1 | 2 | 3 | 4 | 5 |

25. I translate the technical language of my services into the language of benefits that spell out how my firm's services precisely satisfy my client's deepest needs.

    | 1 | 2 | 3 | 4 | 5 |

26. When I present I consciously choose powerful attention-grabbing words that have strong, positive, emotional appeals.

    | 1 | 2 | 3 | 4 | 5 |

27. As I persuade I consciously sell what makes my proposition or ideas unique compared to my competitors.

    | 1 | 2 | 3 | 4 | 5 |

28. I also consciously package my persuasive propositions to appeal to my client's emotional needs.

    | 1 | 2 | 3 | 4 | 5 |

29. I use metaphors, analogies, and stories in my presentations to highlight my key points.

    | 1 | 2 | 3 | 4 | 5 |

30. I consciously limit the number of points I make in any presentation to no more than five.

    | 1 | 2 | 3 | 4 | 5 |

Closing the sale

31. I anticipate objections and deal with them as they occur.

    | 1 | 2 | 3 | 4 | 5 |

32. I never answer objections until I've explored all facets of the objection.

    | 1 | 2 | 3 | 4 | 5 |

33. I consciously test the importance of the objection before offering an answer or solution.

    | 1 | 2 | 3 | 4 | 5 |

34. I preplan and rehearse answers to the most likely objections.

    | 1 | 2 | 3 | 4 | 5 |

35. I watch out, and listen, for positive verbal and nonverbal messages before I attempt to close.

    | 1 | 2 | 3 | 4 | 5 |

36. I check there are no last-minute concerns before I close.

    [1]   [2]   [3]   [4]   [5]

37. I briefly summarize the benefits of working with me before I finally close.

    [1]   [2]   [3]   [4]   [5]

38. Before I make a concession, I calculate what value is the concession to the client, what will it cost me and what do I need in return.

    [1]   [2]   [3]   [4]   [5]

39. I have a negotiation strategy which allows us to trade what is cheap for us for what is valuable for the client.

    [1]   [2]   [3]   [4]   [5]

40. I sell the full value of our services, so I have a built-in margin within the structure of the fee, in case we have to negotiate a fee cut.

    [1]   [2]   [3]   [4]   [5]

Interpreting the Results

The prime purpose of Sales IQ is to help to identify the areas professionals need to improve.

Score	Sales IQ
180–200	**Exceptional:** Professionals who score this high are gifted sellers. They probably need to watch out for complacency.
150–179	**Superior:** This score shows you are a talented seller in many areas but lack the refinements displayed by exceptional sellers.
120–149	**Adequate:** This score indicates you know and practice many of the basics of successful selling. However, you can significantly improve your number of missed opportunities by extending your skills and awareness.
Under 120	**Deficient:** This score indicates your selling skills are weak and need a makeover.

Any professional who scores below 150 urgently needs training in sales and negotiation skills.

SELLING THE VALUE-ADDED SOLUTION

While the best rainmakers may be born, all professionals still need to be able to sell value. It's very difficult, if not impossible, to delight a client if she doesn't appreciate or understand the value of what you are providing in the first place.

WHAT DO BUYERS OF PROFESSIONAL SERVICES PURCHASE?

Before you can successfully sell professional services, you need to understand what buyers of professional services actually buy.

Based on some original work by professional services authority David Maister, we use the Three Es Model to explain how buyers behave when they buy different types of professional services.

The Three Es of buying professional services are Expertise, Experience, and Efficiency. Exhibit 7.2 shows the Three Es Model.

EXHIBIT 7.2

What do buyers of professional services purchase?

The Three Es Model			
	Expertise	Experience	Efficiency
Problem	• Unique • Large • Complex	• Not unique • Can be large • Can be complex	• Common • Large • Simple
Required Solution	I need the expert	I need someone with a track record	I need a proven methodology
Perceived Differentiation	High	Some	Little
Fees	• High • Value driven • Nonnegotiable	• Competitor driven • Negotiable	• Low • Price driven • Work often farmed out

Expertise. When buyers perceive they have a problem that is unique, large, and complex, they search for an expert.

This affects the way you buy. When you hire an expert such as a brain surgeon, you don't bargain, haggle over the fee, or shop around. As a result, experts or gurus can set a fee based on what the market will bear.

Experience. Often buyers feel that they don't need a "brain surgeon," all they need is a "general practitioner." When you go to a GP for advice, the problem is not unique, large, or complex. What you want is help or advice from a professional who has a proven track record doing similar tasks.

Since there is usually a choice of suppliers who have a track record of solving relatively straightforward problems, buyers, if they want to, can shop around. They request quotes from competing suppliers and often negotiate on fees.

Efficiency. When you purchase a professional service that has become a commodity, you are buying an efficiency driven service. When you purchase an efficiency driven service, you are usually buying your supplier's methodology. When clients of an accounting firm purchases an audit, thay are buying the supplier's auditing methodology.

Because buyers believe efficiency driven services are undifferentiated commodities, they buy on price. Buyers of auditing services, for example, typically put their work out for tender, and many play one supplier off against the other.

Lessons from the Three Es

The lessons from the Three Es for sellers of professional services are:
1. When you sell you should always sell and differentiate your expertise. The fees you can charge for expertise can be five to ten times what you charge for efficiency work.

2. Even if you sell largely experience or efficiency driven services, you can command significantly higher margins by offering or embedding expertise driven add-ons.

3. Services over time migrate from expertise to efficiency. Competitors are always looking for ways to simplify and streamline services that require the input of a "expert." So, if you don't keep differentiating your services by adding value and expertise, your service will end up in the efficiency driven column.

THE CLIENT-DRIVEN SELLING PROCESS

Selling is a process of uncovering, developing, and satisfying needs. The sales process or the path to commitment can be broken into four steps:

Step One: Establish your credibility. Step Two: Uncover and develop needs. Step Three: Propose your solution. Step Four: Close the sale.

Step 1: Establish Your Credibility.

The purpose of the initial contact is to:
- Establish your professional credibility
- Create a favorable first impression
- Set your call objectives
- Locate the key decision-makers.

ESTABLISH YOUR PROFESSIONAL CREDIBILITY

It is critical to establish your credibility at the first meeting. The more credible you are in a sale, the more persuasive you are. If the prospects don't believe you're telling the truth, they will discount everything you say.

As a professional:
- First, you have to establish your personal credibility by differentiating yourself.

- Second, you have to establish your firm's credibility by differentiating your firm.
- Third, you have to establish the credibility of your solution by differentiating your ideas and approach.

Remember, once you have established your credibility prospects believe what you say. Until you've established your credibility prospects tend to discount everything you say.

CREATE A FAVORABLE FIRST IMPRESSION

When you meet a prospect for the first time, you have just four minutes to create a positive first impression. If you don't connect with your "first impression," you may never connect.

The tone of an opening discussion is largely determined by your body talk. If your body talk and words contradict each other, clients will believe your body talk.

S-O-F-T-E-N—Remember the acronym **SOFTEN** when you greet your prospect. This will help you keep your body talk positive:

Smile: Smile to generate warmth.
Open stance: Stand with an open posture with your legs apart and arms ready to gesture.
Forward lean: Move your weight forward onto the balls of your feet.
Tone: Vary your voice pitch, rate, and rhythm.
Eye contact: Focus your gaze on the other person's forehead and eyes.
Nod: Punctuate your speech with nods and purposeful gestures.

SET YOUR CALL OBJECTIVES

Before every meeting with a prospect, you should set your call objectives. The results of sales calls can be divided into four types:

- **Close.** This is a call where the customer commits to buying.

- **Advance.** Advance call is one where the customer agrees to specific action that moves the sales forward. For example, the customer sets an appointment for you to talk to another key decision maker.

- **Maintenance.** A maintenance call simply maintains the relationship. There is no progress that advances the sale forward. The customer may, however, agree to continue to have discussions with you.

- **Termination.** Termination occurs where the customer refuses to buy and effectively ends the relationship with no further meetings arranged.

When you plan your sales calls:
- Always plan your call outcomes before the meeting. This provides focus and direction.
- Brainstorm a list of possible call outcomes. Remember that there are multiple ways to advance most sales.
- Aim high when you set your call outcomes. You can always fall back to a less ambitious request.
- State your outcome in terms of a specific action you want the customer to make. Outcomes like "improve the relationship" are too vague to be useful.
- Afterward, assess each meeting against your call outcome. If you failed to advance the sale, ask yourself why.

LOCATE THE DECISION MAKERS

To succeed in the large, more complex sales, you have to identify and sell to all of the parties involved in making the final decision to buy.

In most large sales there are three types of influencers:

- **The Economic Buyer.** This is the financial decision-maker who controls the budget and holds ultimate power over the sale.

- **The User Buyer.** In every sale there are influencers who are responsible for assessing how your product or service will work or operate.

- **Gatekeepers/Technical Screeners.** This group of influencers has the power to block out potential suppliers because their job is to "shortlist" or screen out suppliers, usually on technical grounds. Gatekeepers/Technical Screeners don't have the authority to say yes, but they can say no.

To identify the Economic Buyer, ask: Who has the authority to release the funds for this project?

To identify the User Buyer, ask: Who will use or manage the use or operation of our service?

To identify the Gatekeepers/Technical Screeners, ask: Who are the gatekeepers? Who has the power to screen out potential vendors?

USE A SPONSOR

In a large or complex sale, you need to find a sponsor or guide to help you identify all the decision makers. The ideal sponsor will identify the areas where there is a need for your product or service. They will also have enough influence to recommend that key decision makers set up appointments with you.

Remember, the job of Economic Buyer is sometimes handled by a committee. If it is, try and identify the unofficial leader or dominant influencer.

Allow extra time to gain access to the Financial Buyer. The Financial Buyer often holds the highest position and often has calls screened.

Step Two: Uncover and Develop Needs

Once you have established your credibility with your prospects you can move on to discussing their needs. The art of selling is the ability to uncover customers' problems and turn them into needs for your product or service.

TURNING CLIENT PROBLEMS INTO NEEDS

Customer needs normally start out as minor difficulties or

irritations that over time turn into major problems. They then turn into specific needs or intentions to buy.

Clients typically go through three phases as they become aware that they have a need:

Phase one: Minor concern. The client initially becomes aware he has some minor concerns, irritations, or issues. However, the problem at this stage seems too small to take action.

Phase two: Major problem. The problem has now grown to where it is causing real concern. However, the client still hasn't decided the exact nature of the problem or how to solve it.

Phase three: Specific need. The client has determined what he or she needs to do to solve the problem.

USE THE O-P-E-N QUESTIONING FORMULA

Your most important task while uncovering a prospect's needs is to use questions to turn your prospect's problems into a specific need for your solution. The most persuasive way to do this is to use the persuasive O-P-E-N questioning sequence.

Orientation questions. Top rainmakers start by using background or Orientation questions to gather essential information. These questions help you locate possible problem areas.

Problem questions. With information gathered from the Orientation questions, sellers use Problem questions to expose problems, difficulties, or dissatisfactions.

Effect questions. Top rainmakers then develop or expand the problem in the customer's mind by exploring the consequences, implications, or effects of a customer's problems. These are the keys to disturbing the client and making him or her want to buy.

Need questions. Finally, sellers use Need questions to increase their client's desire for a solution. Need questions get the client to express a clear, stated need and allow the seller to offer a tailored solution.

Exhibit 7.3 summarizes how you use the OPEN questioning process to turn client problems into needs.

EXHIBIT 7.3

The OPEN questioning process

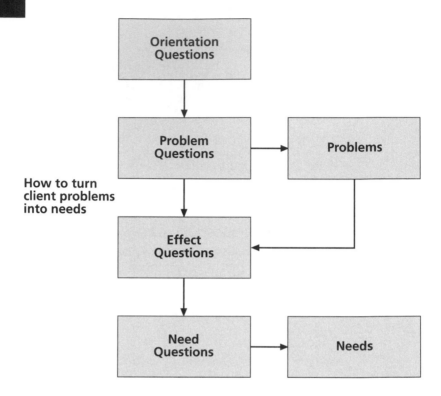

How to turn client problems into needs

RECONCILE PERSONAL AND ORGANIZATIONAL NEEDS

The biggest challenge in step two of the sales cycle is to meet all the buying influences, i.e., the economic buyer, the user buyer, and the technical screener.

When you meet each buying influence, remember that each one has a different list of needs. You also need to keep in mind that every buying influence invariably has two sets of needs to reconcile: (1) their personal needs and (2) the needs of the organization they represent. These two sets of needs sometimes conflict.

EXHIBIT 7.4

Start with Orientation questions

Typical Orientation questions include:

- When did you first establish your business?
- What is your company's ownership structure?
- How long have you been working in this area?
- Who have you used for advice in the past?

Move on to Problem questions

Typical Problem questions include:

- What makes this such a major concern?
- How satisfied are you with . . .?
- How often do you experience problems?
- Who usually bears the blame for the problem?
- What areas do you think could be improved?
- How happy are you with the way . . .?

Disturb with Effect questions

Use these variations of Effect questions to disturb prospects:

- What impact is this problem having on . . .?
- What are the consequences of . . .?
- How will this problem affect your . . .?
- What are the implications of this for . . .?
- How did you feel about that?
- How much do you conservatively estimate this problem has cost you?

Move to the solution with Need questions

Use Need questions to create buyer commitment:

- What benefits would there be if we could help you to reduce . . .?
- How much could you save if we get rid of the . . . fees?
- How would it help if we could reduce the down time?
- Why is it important to solve this problem?

Here is a relationship matrix to help you assess the strength and nature of the relationship you hold with each buying influence.

EXHIBIT 7.5

Strength of relationship matrix

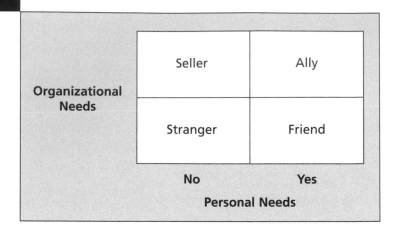

If you don't know what buyers' organizational or personal needs are, you are a *stranger*.

If you know buyers' organizational needs but don't know what their personal needs are, you are a *vendor* or *seller*.

If you know buyers' personal needs but don't know what their organizational needs are, you are a *friend*.

If you know buyers' personal needs and also know their organizational needs you are an *ally*.

Top rainmakers use their relationship and persuasion skills to turn strangers, friends and sellers into allies.

Step Three: Propose Solutions

Once you've uncovered your prospects' needs, you are ready to present your solution. In step three you match the features and benefits of your services to your clients' needs and establish your superiority over the competition.

FOCUS ON BENEFITS

Now that you have uncovered your buyers' needs, you are in a position to propose or sell what your service can do.

Compare the appeal of the promotion "apples contain vitamins and natural sugar" with "an apple a day keeps the doctor away." The first promotion describes facts or features about the apple, the second promotion describes how the apple will help the buyer. The second promotion sells the benefits of what the apple can do.

Features are the facts that describe what a product or service is and how it is made or works. Benefits describe how the product or service will help the prospect.

Features are cold, remote, and impersonal; benefits are warm and tempting. While prospects can be interested in features, it is benefits that cement the sale.

CUSTOMIZE THE BENEFITS

Benefits will have little impact on your sales unless you customize and tailor them to meet your customers' precise needs.

Here is an example of a consultant tailoring her service to a concerned client:

"You said that you were particularly concerned about the costs of the high levels of inventory you're having to carry. Our inventory planning process will allow you to cut your carrying costs by 17 percent to 28 percent."

Notice how the consultant has:
- Used the phrase "you said that" to prove to the customer she has been listening to his concerns.
- Used the client's exact words to describe her concern. Customers will never argue about their own words.
- Customized her service's features and benefits.

To become a master at benefit selling:
- Preface all your benefits statements with the phrase "you said

that." Then use the customers' exact words to state their concern before selling your features and benefits.

- Push the benefits that set your services apart in the market place. These are the ones that will give you a competitive edge.
- Where possible use independent third-party endorsements to support your claims. Most clients are sceptical until offered proof.
- Listen for the buyer to say: "that's exactly what I want." This confirms you are on the right track.
- Ask your buyers to state the benefits of your solution. Benefits that come from the buyers' mouths are much more persuasive.

OUTFLANK YOUR COMPETITORS

To succeed as a seller you must have a detailed knowledge of your competitor's strengths and weaknesses. You become exposed when a competitor is strong in an area where you are weak and that is critical to the customer. There is a simple way to assess your vulnerability. Called competitive analysis, it is illustrated in Exhibit 7.6.

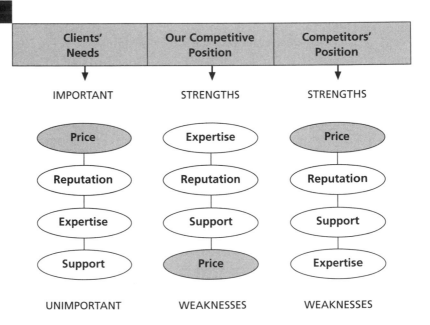

EXHIBIT 7.6

Competitive analysis

Clients' Needs	Our Competitive Position	Competitors' Position
IMPORTANT	STRENGTHS	STRENGTHS
Price	Expertise	Price
Reputation	Reputation	Reputation
Expertise	Support	Support
Support	Price	Expertise
UNIMPORTANT	WEAKNESSES	WEAKNESSES

In the example shown, you are weak on support compared to your competitor. The result is that you are highly vulnerable. If you don't act to overcome your weaknesses you will lose the sale.

THE THREE COMPETITIVE STRATEGIES

Once you have used competitive analysis to compare yourself to the competition, you can plan your approach. There are three strategies.

Strategy one: Sell

Your first task is to use your sales skills to get the customers to change their buying criteria, particularly in those areas where you are weaker than the competition. On the competitive analysis chart, you are trying to influence the left-hand scale. In the example shown in Exhibit 7.6, your sales goal is to reduce the importance of price in the prospect's mind while stressing the critical importance of expertise and reputation.

Strategy two: Negotiate

To further reduce your vulnerability, you can negotiate with the buyer. Typically, this means trading concessions. On the competitive analysis chart, you are trying to influence the middle scale. In the example illustrated, you might have to make some price concessions to close the sale.

Strategy three: Expose and outflank your competitors

Here you use your research to compare yourself to the competitors. You acknowledge your competitors' strengths but also point out their weaknesses and in the process raise doubts as to whether they can meet your client's crucial buying criteria. In the example shown, you need to subtly expose your competitors' lack of expertise.

Step Four: Close the Sale

Having proposed your solution, all you now have to do is establish the prospects' commitment by closing the sale.

In this final step you:
- Monitor your clients' buying signals
- Overcome any objections
- Close the sale.

TEST YOUR PROSPECT'S COMMITMENT WITH TRIAL CLOSES

As you move through the sales process, you need to regularly check that your customer is advancing toward closure. Trial closes are questions that check your prospect's "buying temperature" and verify that the prospect remains interested.

Here are five typical trial closes:
- *"Does our proposed timetable meet your requirements?"*
- *"Does our approach fit in with your thinking?"*
- *"How will your people feel about the changes the new system will produce?"*
- *"Is there anything you would like me to go over again?"*
- *"What advantages do you see in using this approach?"*

If the prospect reacts positively to your trial closes, you can move to the next step in your sale. If the prospect reacts negatively, treat the reaction as an objection and a request for more information.

Use trial closes:
- When presenting each major feature or benefit
- After handling and overcoming an objection
- When you observe a buying signal.

USE THE *Feel-Felt-Found* STRATEGY TO HANDLE NEGATIVE REACTIONS:

1st F: "I understand how you *feel* . . ."
2nd F: "Lots of my clients have *felt* the same way . . ."
3rd F: "They *found* that . . ." (then recall the benefit)

Handling Objections

Anticipate and overcome objections. The rainmaker who encounters large numbers of objections toward the end of the sales process has usually not done the job properly. If you've uncovered a client's needs properly and provided a tailored solution, there should be very few last-minute objections.

Even so, you do still have to be adept at anticipating and answering objections. The key to answering objections is to deal with them when they are small—well before they become major stumbling blocks.

Never ignore objections. Whenever you hear an objection, acknowledge it—never ignore it. And don't answer it until you fully understand what lies behind the customer's concerns.

Behind many client objections are unexpressed or unidentified needs. With sensitive, systematic questioning you can use objection handling to deepen your rapport with the customer.

The Five-Step Close

Handling objections is a five-step process.
1. Listen to the objection. Never interrupt the customer.
2. Acknowledge and convey your concern even when you don't agree with the objection.
3. Explore the nature of the concern. Question to establish unidentified needs.
4. Test to check the importance of the objection. Establish whether it is a minor or major concern.
5. Answer the objection. Then confirm that the customer is satisfied.

WHEN TO CLOSE

Top rainmakers look and listen for verbal and nonverbal signals that the client is ready to buy. The most common buying signals include:

* *Positive body talk.* A client moves from a negative to a positive body posture and smiles or nods in agreement.

- *Statements or questions that indicate the customer is ready to close.* The client's talk shifts from a discussion about the product to specific details or costs, delivery times or ongoing service, and how installation would be carried out.

When the client sends out these signals, it is time to close. The easiest way to test whether your timing is right is to say to the customer, *"We seem to be close to an agreement. Do you have any remaining concerns?"* If the customer replies, *"No, I think you've covered everything,"* follow through with the rest of the close.

HOW TO CLOSE

Closing is a four-step process. The first letters of each step form the acronym **WASP.**

- **W**atch out for positive verbal and nonverbal signals. Listen especially for questions on delivery or implementation.
- **A**nswer any remaining concerns; ask, "Is there anything else I need to cover?"
- **S**ummarize the benefits. Focus on the two or three benefits that will provide most of the value.
- **P**ropose an appropriate commitment. Spell out exactly what you want the client to commit to.

NEGOTIATING TO RETAIN MARGIN

If you sell well, i.e., you sell the full value of what you have to offer, you can negotiate with clients from a position of strength. Even so, the best firms don't leave the final results to chance. A U.K. accountancy benchmark survey reports the top firms are twice as likely to field staff trained in negotiation techniques as their less successful counterparts.[6]

How do you handle a buyer who is pressuring you for a discount? The answer very much depends on the type of buyer. Essentially there are two types of buyers: relationship buyers and transaction buyers, and each one requires a different approach.

Negotiating with Transaction Buyers

As the title suggests, the prime concern of transaction buyers is price. Where can they they make the buying process as competitive as possible? Transaction driven negotiators love "sealed bids" and are notorious for resisting attempts to refocus their attention on value.

It's highly tempting to think you can convert a transaction buyer into a value motivated relationship buyer. But before you try, always consider the old tale about the frog and the scorpion.

> The scorpion asks the frog for a ride across the river. "No way" says the frog, "You'll sting me and I'll die."
> "But that doesn't make sense," replies the scorpion. "If I sting you I'll drown too. It's against both our interests."
> Convinced, the frog gives the scorpion a ride. Of course, half way across the river the scorpion stings the frog.
> "Why did you do that," gasps the dying frog.
> "It's my nature," says the scorpion.

It is possible to convert transaction buyers into relationship buyers, but like the scorpion, most transaction buyers never change. It's their nature. So beware!

Here are the key tips on how to negotiate with a transaction buyer who plays hardball.

Walk away from unprofitable deals
Don't fall into the trap of cutting your price in anticipation of further profits. Experience shows they rarely materialize. So, if you can't make money from the current deal, walk away.

Use a BATNA to create leverage
Before you start negotiating work out your BATNA. A BATNA is your *Best Alternative to a Negotiated Agreement*. When you work out your BATNA, you are calculating your walk away position.

Sell before you trade
Don't quote or discuss price until you have sold your total package with all the bells and whistles added in.

Strenuously resist all attempts to quote indicative prices until you've completed your presentation. When aggressive buyers push you to give a "ball park" price, simply assure them your price will be highly competitive.

Prioritize your tradables

Before you start negotiating, prepare a list of tradables. Rank your needs into three groups based on priority.

- *High Priority*. Your *must* gets. These are your essentials. If you don't achieve these, walk away.
- *Medium Priority*. Your *should* gets. The deal does not satisfy your minimum interests. You expect to achieve these.
- *Low Priority*. Your *could* gets. You would like to achieve these. These are your tradables.

Remember, the essence of skillful bargaining is to trade what is cheap for you for what is valuable for the other side.

Start high, concede slowly

With price buyers it pays to adopt a hardline bargaining strategy. When you make an offer, give yourself plenty of room to negotiate. A high opening position however should always be realistic and credible. If you can't justify your demand, don't make it. Ridiculous demands simply generate hostility.

Link issues

Before you start trading concessions, get all of the other party's demands on the table. Then make it clear that any concession on any one item is conditional upon agreement on the other outstanding issues.

Avoid making the first major concession

If you can, get the other party to make the first concession, especially on a major issue. Research shows that losers generally make the first concessions on major issues. So if you do have to make the first concession to get momentum going, make it on a minor issue.

Control your concession rate

Winning negotiators control their concession rate much better than losers do. Successful negotiators make smaller concessions, are less generous, and less predictable. And they don't crack under deadline pressure.

Trade reluctantly

Make the other side toil for every concession they get. Price negotiators value concessions they have to work for.

Make small concessions

Don't give large concessions. Instead, give a series of small ones. Successful bargainers make consistently smaller concessions than their opponents.

Be patient—concede slowly

Negotiators who move too fast easily lose control. Quick negotiators are characterized by rapid concession-making, which is invariably disastrous for one side or the other.

Conserve your concessions

Don't give away your concessions too early. Be prepared to make the other party wait. They appreciate them more. Since you often need a concession or two to close a deal, you should always hold some concessions in reserve.

Demand reciprocation

Never give away a concession without getting a concession in return. Don't give away anything for nothing. Everything should be conceded in exchange for something else.

Make all concessions conditional

To protect yourself from giving away free concessions, preface all your offers with a condition. Use the if/then formula. "*If* you agree to A, *then* I will agree to B."

Justify all concessions

Don't give away concessions without supporting justification.

Track all concessions

As you keep track of all the offers and concessions, patterns should emerge that give insights into your opponent's priorities.

When under attack, listen

Don't become sidetracked by emotion-driven attacks. Keep the prospect talking and listen hard for fresh information that will create room for movement.

Assert your firm's needs

For a deal to work it must satisfy your needs as well as theirs. Hardball negotiators act as though there is only one set of needs—theirs. So don't be afraid to state clearly what you want, feel, and think.

Don't cave into dirty tactics

Some hardball negotiators use dirty tactics to gain an upper hand. At the very least, most hardball negotiators misrepresent what they can afford to pay and exaggerate or disguise facts to strengthen their position.

Here are your tactical options:
- *Ignore the tactic.* Simply recognizing a negative tactic strengthens your hand.
- *Call the tactic.* Describing the negative tactic and calmly stating why you think it is unproductive will often cause the other party to reassess its approach.
- *Walk away.* Toxic clients are rarely worth the hassle.
- *Retaliate with your own counter tactics.* Beware! This is high risk and often backfires.

Negotiating with Relationship Buyers

Relationship buyers want to expand the pie and build a win-win agreement. They like to problem solve and are often prepared to discuss long-term as well as short-term needs.

Emphasize the value of the solution against the size of the problem

Because relationship buyers are solution rather than price driven, they listen and usually respond to presentations that clearly demonstrate the advantages of working with you.

Sell the long-term benefits of working with you

The real insights and breakthroughs you can offer often require an intimate working relationship. Subtly remind the client that this takes time.

Focus on interests not positions

Don't haggle over positions. Before you ever talk price or take a position, make sure you understand the client's interests or underlying needs.

To identify the clients' interests, list all the points you want them to agree to. Then ask: *what might stop them* agreeing to your request? The answers will very likely include their interests.

Adopt a moderate opening position

In a value-based, relationship-focused negotiation, it rarely pays to open aggressively with an extreme demand. Set a fair fee and make sure it is based on objective criteria.

Package your offer as a bundled offer

If you can, package an offer as a bundle of complementary or related services. "Unbundling," i.e., removing services from your bundle, allows you to reduce your price while maintaining the integrity of your initial price.

Stress goal alignment

Win-win collaborative negotiations are based on goal alignment. Both sides search for ways to align their goals so both can gain.

Become a collaborative problem solver

Joint problem solving for mutual gain forms the basis of a win-win negotiation.

Collaborative problem solving is a four-step process.
Step 1: Jointly define the problem
Step 2: Identify the underlying needs and interests
Step 3: Generate multiple options
Step 4: Agree on the best solution.

For relationship negotiating to work, both parties must be willing to collaborate. If one side plays hardball or engages in deception, the deal will quickly sour.

WRITING A WINNING SALES PROPOSAL

In most large sales you will be asked to submit a proposal. The successful proposal is client focused, differentiates you from the competition, and sells the value of what you have to offer. It is always surprising how often failed sales are the result of a boiler plate proposal that confirms to the clients you don't really understand their special concerns.

Use a Six-Part Persuasive Structure

Here is a six-part persuasive structure for you to use and adapt.

1. **Buyer's needs**

   Your proposal should begin with a list of your prospect's needs ranked in order of importance.

2. **Your recommendations**

   Your recommendations should show how you will solve the prospect's problems and should sell the benefits of your solution.

3. **Why your firm?**

   This section should explain why you should be the provider of first choice. Stress what sets you apart from your competitors.

4. **Your guarantee**

   Offer a guarantee if you can. An unconditional warranty on your product or service is a powerful persuader.

5. **The rationale behind your pricing**

   If possible, include a graphic cost/benefit analysis.

6. **Your current clients/endorsements**

   List your current clients and include relevant endorsements from delighted customers.

The One-Read Test

If you can't skim-read your proposals and take in all the key points in one read, then it is very likely your staff urgently need training in effective writing.

Use the checklist in Exhibit 7.7 to assess the quality of your sales proposals.

EXHIBIT 7.7

Check that your written sales proposal:	✔	✘
• Is organized logically	☐	☐
• Is written from the client's point of view	☐	☐
• Stresses benefits over features	☐	☐
• Uses words and phrases that sell	☐	☐
• Uses headings to announce key points	☐	☐
• Sells the value of your offer	☐	☐
• Differentiates you from competitors	☐	☐
• Establishes your credentials	☐	☐
• Offers verifiable proof to support any claims	☐	☐
• Uses graphs and diagrams to demonstrate key points	☐	☐
• Uses reader-friendly language—short words, short sentences, and short paragraphs.	☐	☐

DELIVERING A COMPELLING SALES PRESENTATION

The U.K.–based accountancy benchmark survey discovered that the winning accounting firms in their survey (those who won more than 50 percent of their bids) were much more likely to:

- Train their team in presentation techniques
- Provide a detailed proposal document
- Include team members who'll work on the project
- Support their presentation with visual aids
- Prepare scripts or notes for presenters
- Include a senior partner on their bid team
- Allow time for questions.[7]

All successful rainmakers have to be able to deliver a compelling sales presentation. A persuasive presentation is often the difference between success and failure.

THE SEVEN-STEP PERSUASION SEQUENCE

Persuasive sales presentations are built around a seven-step persuasion sequence. Follow these steps and you will dramatically increase the number of sales you close.

EXHIBIT 7.8

The seven-step persuasion sequence

Problem	Effect	Need	Recommendations	Benefits	Differentiation	Credentials
Identify the problem	Quantify the impact of the problem	Specify the need	Propose your solution	Quantify the value	Sell your competitive advantage	Substantiate your claims
1	2	3	4	5	6	7

Step 1: Identify the problem

When you identify problems in a sales presentation, make sure you focus on the problems you can solve. Don't talk about issues you can't resolve.

Step 2: Quantify the impact of the problem

Clients won't spend money on problems that are insignificant or represent minor irritations. The ideal problem is: large, complex, and urgent.

Remember the 5 to 1 problem-to-fee ratio. This ratio states that the problem needs to be five times the size of the fee. In other words, a $100,000 problem will sustain a $20,000 fee.

Step 3: Specify the need

Here you spell out what the client needs. Personalize and tailor the analysis by using the words of the prospect's decision-maker.

Step 4: Recommend your solution

Propose an easy-to-follow step-by-step plan. This is the time in your presentation to generate discussion by calling for questions. If you can, support your recommendation by citing a comparable success story.

Step 5: Quantify the benefits

Prospects are impressed if you can quantify the benefits. If you are promising higher margins, spell out what figures the client can expect to achieve. But be careful not to exaggerate.

Step 6: Differentiate yourself

Explain what makes you different from your competitors. Sell your unique value proposition (UVP) by highlighting your strengths. Be prepared to discuss your competitors, but show respect and at all times strive to be super objective.

Step 7: Establish your credentials

Finish your presentation with third-party endorsements and testimonials. The best testimonials come from organizations the prospect admires. Personal endorsements supported by specific figures are especially powerful.

Follow this seven-step sequence, and you'll see your success rate climb rapidly.

Win-Loss Reports

Do you compile win/loss reports to analyze why you win or lose competitive bids? You should! Can you imagine a professional sports team not analyzing why it wins or loses every game it plays?

The best way to get client feedback after a presentation is a face-to-face interview or a telephone call. Clients are much more reluctant to put negative feedback on paper.

The purpose of a win/loss interview is to assess your strengths and weaknesses as compared to your competitors.

You have to be persuasive and persistent when you ask clients to spend time with you after you've just lost a bid. Explain you're in this "for the long term" and their feedback is essential if you are to come back better in the next round.

THE WIN-LOSS INTERVIEW PROCESS

Start with broad, general, open-ended probes. Ask:

- What was critical to you when you made your buying decision?
- What special abilities did Firm X offer compared to the competition?
- Could you please rank your priorities from top to bottom?

Now probe deeper. Ask:

- How did we compare to our competitors on each of your key selection criteria?

To make win/loss reporting work you need to:

1. Complete interviews immediately after the win or loss. Feedback has to be fresh to be of any practical use.
2. Debrief on wins as well as losses. It's just as important, if not more, to understand why you won and know what areas you still need to improve.
3. Share the debriefs with all of the team. But edit out negative comments on individuals. These should be delivered in private.
4. Draft a corrective plan of action.
5. Prepare a periodic analysis summarizing the recurring patterns behind your wins and losses.

EXHIBIT 7.9

Proposal/presentation win/loss an analysis

Win-Loss Report							
Period:							
Total No.		No. Won		No. Lost		Success Rate	%
Est. Value		Est. Value		Est. Value		Previous Period Success Rate	%
Critical Success Factors (List 1–5)							
1.							
2.							
3.							
4.							
5.							
Critical Loss Factors (List 1–5)							
1.							
2.							
3.							
4.							
5.							
Actions Required							

Rainmaking success needs to be monitored, measured, and analyzed.

The Sales Performance Analysis form gives you the essential information you need to measure the efficiency and effectiveness of your selling efforts.

EXHIBIT 7.10

Sales performance analysis

	Plan	Actual	%
Total Sales			
Sales revenues			
Average sale size			
Successful closes %			
New Clients			
Total sales revenues			
Number of sales			
Average sales size			
Calls per sale			
Formal proposals			
Full presentations			
Successful closes %			
Existing Clients			
Sales			
Number of sales			
Average sales size			
Calls per sale			
Formal proposals			
Full presentations			
Successful closes %			

ACTION

STEPS

1. Use the Sales IQ to assess the sales competencies of all your professionals.

2. Establish a common sales language across your firm by training all your staff in sales and influencing skills.

3. Establish a sales monitoring process to track the progress of prospects through the sales cycle.

4. Assess your sales proposals against the criteria in the six-part persuasive structure.

5. Set up a win-loss bid reporting system to analyze your staff performance in competitive bids.

6. Train all your professional staff in the key rainmaking competencies: selling, negotiating, and presenting.

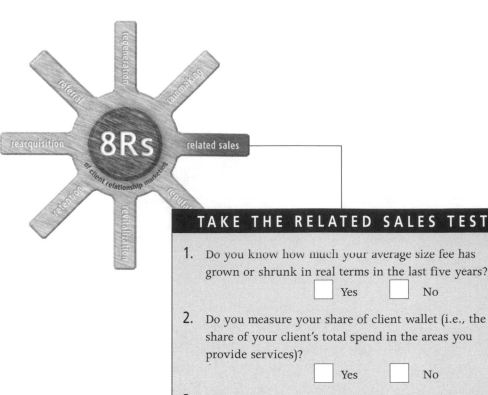

TAKE THE RELATED SALES TEST

1. Do you know how much your average size fee has grown or shrunk in real terms in the last five years?
   ☐ Yes   ☐ No

2. Do you measure your share of client wallet (i.e., the share of your client's total spend in the areas you provide services)?
   ☐ Yes   ☐ No

3. Do you measure what percentage of each fee-earner's income comes from cross-selling?
   ☐ Yes   ☐ No

4. Do you know how many services your typical client purchases?
   ☐ Yes   ☐ No

5. Do you know how many services your typical high value client buys?
   ☐ Yes   ☐ No

6. Have your partners and senior staff been trained to up-sell and cross-sell?
   ☐ Yes   ☐ No

7. Do you have a plan to up-sell and cross-sell additional service to your high potential clients?
   ☐ Yes   ☐ No

8. Do you convert your core expertise into additional income streams such as seminars, publications, and software?
   ☐ Yes   ☐ No

CHAPTER **8**

RELATED SALES

*How to grow your revenues
and margins by up-selling and
cross-selling*

Features

- Selling profitable add-ons
- How to identify profitable add-ons
- The three types of cross-selling
- How to up-sell and cross-sell for additional revenue
- Monitoring your cross-selling efforts
- Action steps

SELLING PROFITABLE ADD-ONS

There are two ways to grow existing clients: You can up-sell, i.e., increase the size of your average fee, or you can cross-sell or multiply the number of products/services you sell.

One in Four Clients Has Upgrade Potential

The potential for up-selling and cross-selling is enormous. Our experience across a variety of practices indicates one in four clients has the upgrade potential. The big qualification here, however, is it's much more difficult to upgrade small clients with limited budgets.

BUYERS OF MULTIPLE SERVICES ARE MORE LOYAL

Banking research shows that the more products a customer purchases, the less likely a customer is to defect. We've found a similar pattern with many professional service firms. The more services you supply, the more likely a client is to stay loyal.

Providing multiple services allows you to broaden and deepen your relationship. As your buying network within an organization expands, you find you are no longer so dependent on the goodwill of just one or two individuals for your continued supply of work. Finally, it is much more difficult to dispose of a service provider when something goes wrong if you are dependent on it for a wide range of services.

THE LITTLER MENDELSON EXAMPLE

One of the best professional service practices we've observed at creating and selling integrated add-ons is the U.S. employment and labor law firm Littler Mendelson (www.Littler.com).

Littler Mendelson, with 441 attorneys in 31 offices, is the largest law firm in the United States, practicing exclusively in employment and labor law, representing management.

Littler's attorneys offer three core services:
1. It acts as an *extension* to a company's in-house legal department.
2. It acts as a *full-service employment* law counsel.
3. It *trains* human resource supervisors and managers in employment law. Its seminar programs include annual Employer Conferences and Breakfast Briefings.

Its publications include employer handbooks and in-depth task force reports, newsletters, and videos. Littler Mendelson's Legal Learning Group runs programs that range from instructor-led separate training to distance learning via the Internet and satellite.

With this range of services and products, Littler Mendelson can bundle its services in multiple ways. For example, for a fee of $1,175, you can join the Littler Passport™ Program. The passport entitles you to a national employer conference, breakfast briefings, task force reports, and A.S.A.P. newsletters.

HOW TO IDENTIFY PROFITABLE ADD-ONS

If you always keep in mind what your client ultimately wants to achieve with your service, you can nearly always come up with profitable add-on products and services. The first question to ask when considering how to increase your add-on services is: How can we get our clients to increase the volume and frequency of their purchases?

Jay Abraham, in *Getting Everything You Can Out of All You've Got,* offers four valuable ways to help create profitable add-ons. Abraham advises:

1. "Observe what your clients do before they buy your goods or services." Ask, can you also provide that service? Lots of times the provision of a professional service is preceded by a needs analysis or audit. Ask, can you provide that service as well?

2. "Watch what people themselves do with your service after they buy it." A training company provides coaching and mentoring services to the salespeople it trains on its courses. Ask, what follow-through services can you provide?

3. "See what the people buy to go with your product or service in the pursuit of your end result." It makes sense for you to purchase the hardware or software if you provide the service to install and maintain it. Wherever possible try to deepen the relationship.

4. "Ask yourself how you would make a client's end result even more complete."[1] Our training company doesn't just train our clients in sales and negotiation. We help clients strategize and close their largest deals.

THE THREE TYPES OF CROSS-SELLING

Cross-selling opportunities come in three forms:
- You can cross-sell to an unrelated need.
- You can cross-sell sequentially—upstream and downstream.
- You can sell an integrated solution.

CROSS-SELLING TO AN UNRELATED NEED

This happens when a professional working in one area tries to sell the firm's services into a totally new, unrelated area. Cross-selling to an unrelated area is always difficult because you can't use the expertise in the area you are currently working in to establish leverage.

CROSS-SELLING SEQUENTIALLY

Selling upstream and downstream, as it is sometimes called, is a much easier sell because of the close and logical links that exist between the current service and the new one.

Much of the knowledge, insights, and experience you gain from your initial work can be recycled on the subsequent project. It therefore makes perfect sense for an accountant who manages a client's taxes to help the same client set up the financial controls to prevent future problems.

CROSS-SELLING AN INTEGRATED SOLUTION

This works where the client's problem requires a multidisciplined approach. The megasized firms have expanded because they know clients increasingly have problems no one service can solve.

Some clients prefer to use a single supplier who can deliver a full skill set required for an integrated solution. Accountability issues are much easier to resolve if there is just one supplier.

Look for Wedge Projects

Wedge projects are usually small projects that give you a small foothold inside a promising client's organization.

The ideal wedge project allows you to:
- Establish your credibility
- Demonstrate your expertise
- Locate further opportunities
- Understand the client's decision-making process.

Many professional firms give away or heavily discount their wedge projects. Their pitch is, "give us a chance to show you what we can do . . . and it won't cost you much."

The problem with this approach is that clients don't value what they don't pay for. It's much better to charge a reasonable fee, deliver a stunning solution, and follow through with exceptional service.

HOW TO UP-SELL AND CROSS-SELL

At first glance, the quickest way to rapidly grow fees in a multidisciplinary practice is to cross-sell. Why then do so many professional firms struggle to cross-sell?

Reason 1: Professionals too often treat their clients as their personal or practice group's private property. This protective attitude is compounded by incentive systems that encourage professionals to focus all their selling energies on increasing their own department revenues instead of promoting the larger firm.

Recommended solution: Change compensation systems so staff are rewarded to cross-selling. Improve the goodwill and increase trust by making the parties work on common projects. Team-building training also helps.

Reason 2: Many professional practices remain siloed into separate practice groups. There is a separate litigation department, an employment law practice, a separate commercial law practice, and so on.

When staff work in geographically separate specialist departments, cross-selling usually suffers. When it comes to cross-selling, professionals do not sell other parts of their firm; they sell fellow professionals within their firm whom they know and trust.

Staff who don't know each other or don't work together find it hard to cross-sell each other. The downside risk is simply too great.

Recommended solution: If it's not possible to overcome the problem of geographically separate departments by grouping people in industry or common client groups, then special efforts have to be made to get the parties to know and trust each other.

We've found team training or sales training will help the parties come together to build trust and rapport.

Reason 3: Staff don't know anything or enough about the capabilities of other parts of the firm. Professionals will not talk about, let alone recommend, areas or disciplines they know little or nothing about. And as firms get larger this problem escalates.

Recommended solution: Most firms need to double or triple the information flow and training time they spend updating staff on what is happening "across the practice."

Reason 4: When most professionals sell and deliver services they focus most of their promotional efforts on, first, selling themselves, second, selling their departmental expertise, and, finally, if at all, their firm. It's hardly surprising that a client who suddenly needs a valuation fails to call in the firm that has provided expertise in indirect tax for the last fifteen years.

Recommended solution: Continually promote among your staff your firm's brand and the core values and competencies that distinguish you from competitors.

Reason 5: Staff too often try to sell services that have little to do with or are totally unrelated to the service they currently provide. Cross-selling works best when you sell services that are a natural extension or a logical complement to the service you currently provide. It's not surprising that a lot of tax work flows out of the audit work of an accounting practice. They go together like ham and cheese.

Recommended solution: Identify the core areas that create most of the opportunities for cross-selling and training staff intensively in those areas of "natural extension" (Exhibit 8.1).

EXHIBIT 8.1

**Cross-sell into
areas of natural
extension**

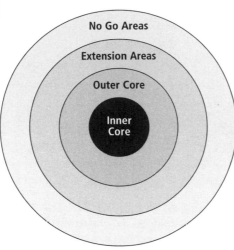

No Go Areas
Involvement would
seriously damage and
compromise reputation

Extension Areas
Areas to which practice
can be widened without
damage

Outer Core
Easiest areas to cross-sell
into

Inner Core
Core business

Poor Sales Technique Is a Huge Problem

The prime cause why cross-selling fails is, however, the fact that
most professionals simply don't know how to cross-sell.

To effectively cross-sell you have to be able to prove to a client
that:

1. You have an understanding of the issues facing the area into
   which you are trying to cross-sell.
2. You can demonstrate how your firm can add value in that area.
3. You have a working knowledge of the expertise of other
   firm/team members you are trying to cross-sell.
4. You can recall specific examples of what the team or expert you
   are trying to cross-sell has achieved for particular clients.
5. There is value in using a practice that can offer an "integrated
   range" of services.

Failed Attempt to Cross-sell

If you were the customer, how would you react to this attempt at
cross-selling?

Partner: *I hear you're looking to install a new customer
             relationship management (CRM) software system.*

Client:	Yes. We have been looking at the ways we can bring together all the information we have on our clients into one centrally coordinated sales information system. We've already begun the consultancy selection process.
Partner:	You may not appreciate we have a team that specializes in this area—our CRM Division. You should meet Paul Kelly, who heads the team. I'm sure it would be worth your while.
Client:	Possibly, but we really are in a hurry. We've already spent a lot of time drawing up a short list. What can you do that the likes of Siebel and Oracle cannot?
Partner:	Well, Paul Kelly is also an expert in this area. He came to us with a long track record in installing sales automation and customer relationship management systems. I'm sure a half an hour's time with Paul would be worth your while.
Client:	Perhaps. Look why don't you get Paul to send me an outline of what you do. If it looks promising we will arrange a meeting.

This attempt to cross-sell has, for all practical purposes, failed. Now read the successful attempt and notice the differences.

Successful Attempt to Cross-sell

Partner:	I hear you're looking to install a new customer relationship management (CRM) software system.
Client:	Yes. We have been looking at the ways we can bring together all the information we have on our clients into one centrally coordinated sales information system. We've already begun the consultancy selection process.
Partner:	You may not appreciate that we have a team that specializes in this area—our CRM Division. You should meet Paul Kelly, who heads the team. I'm sure it would be worth your while.
Client:	Possibly, but we really are in a hurry. We've already spent a lot of time drawing up a short list. What can

you do that the likes of Siebel and Oracle cannot?

Partner:	*Paul Kelly has worked on Oracle and Siebel systems for some years. The reason we brought Paul to head our team was because he knows the strengths and weaknesses of all the main players in CRM, he has worked with the likes of Unilever and BMW, and he can give you independent, unbiased advice.*
	Just as importantly, Paul will be able to save time by building on the work we did in documenting your back-office information systems last year. Working together, we could create one seamless information system.
Client:	*That makes sense. Get Paul to arrange an appointment with my secretary.*
Partner:	*I would like to attend that meeting as well, if I may. That way I can more easily understand what we need to do to maximize the value to you.*

Did you notice that in the successful attempt to cross-sell:

- The partner had detailed understanding of Paul's expertise.
- The partner could differentiate Paul from the competition.
- The partner clearly sold the benefits of meeting with Paul.
- The partner sold the value of growing the relationship with the firm.
- The partner showed he was personally committed to working with Paul to realize the benefits for the client.

We've created a form called the Related Sales Opportunity Assessment (Exhibit 8.2). Use it whenever you identify a promising opportunity.

MONITORING YOUR CROSS-SELLING EFFORTS

Most professional firms rely on anecdotal evidence for much of the information they use to judge the success of their cross-selling efforts. To accurately judge your efforts you need to monitor and measure:

- The names and numbers of the services you provide to every high value or high potential value client.

EXHIBIT 8.2

Related sales opportunity assessment

Client:
Opportunity: Describe Estimate Potential Revenue
Ability to Compete: Strengths Weaknesses
Likely Competitor(s): Strengths Weaknesses
Chances of Success: Estimate Odds Explain
Cross-Sell Strategy: Personnel Resources Tactics

- The total value of the services your high value or high value potential clients purchase in the areas you compete for work.
- The share of that work you win—sometimes called the "share of client wallet."

Skillful surveying of clients will give most of the information you need here. If you can, try and find out the value of the services and the share of client wallet your key competitors have with your high value clients and prospects. Most clients are reluctant to reveal this. But it's worth a try.

1. Set up measures to record:
   - The names and numbers of services you provide to each high value client
   - The share of each client's high value or high potential value work (share of wallet) you win in the areas in which you compete
   - The share of wallet your key competitors have in each of your high value clients
   - Each high value or high potential value client for up-sell and cross-sell potential.

2. Train all professional staff how to cross-sell.

3. Review the cultural and organizational and compensation barriers that currently exist to successful up-selling and cross-selling.

4. Review the ways you can raise the knowledge and awareness everyone has of all your firm's services.

5. Set up a team to identify profitable add-ons by asking the question, *"How can we get our clients to increase the size and frequency of their purchases?"*

TAKE THE REPUTATION BUILDING TEST

1. Can your clients readily describe your brand (practice identity) in a way that clearly distinguishes your firm from its key competitors?

   ☐ Yes ☐ No

2. Does your branding and positioning allow you to command a price premium in your key markets?

   ☐ Yes ☐ No

3. Does your branding reflect the expectations, personality, and self-image of your best clients?

   ☐ Yes ☐ No

4. Would you describe your firm's brand as its largest bankable asset?

   ☐ Yes ☐ No

5. Do you continually educate/train your staff in what your brand stands for in terms of value and service?

   ☐ Yes ☐ No

CHAPTER 9

REPUTATION BUILDING

How to brand your practice to attract premium business

Features

- Building a powerful brand
- The six dimensions of brand identity
- How to clarify your brand identity
- The power of archetypes
- Let me tell you a story
- Developing a brand persona
- Plan for the long term
- To advertise or not to advertise
- Action steps

BUILDING A POWERFUL BRAND

In most industries companies that have strong brands outperform those that don't. A Citibank study found companies with well-known brands outperformed the stock market average by between 15 and 20 percent over a fifteen-year period.

For professional service companies who sell intangibles, brand identity is even more important than it is for product-driven companies.

However, we have to say money spent on branding activities in a professional service firm will rarely add value unless the firm already has a foundation of quality differentiated services in place.

The success formula is: quality services plus differentiation enhanced by branding equals sustained competitive advantage.

The Bottom-line Benefits of a Strong Brand

For a professional service firm, its brand can be its largest bankable asset. A strong brand:

- Attracts and retains clients
- Simplifies buying decisions
- Differentiates the firm from competitors
- Makes it much easier for a firm to expand into new markets
- Increases margins.

There has been an upsurge in branding activity among professional firms in recent years. The Legal Marketing Association's (LMA) 2001 survey of law firm marketing budgets showed that 51 percent of respondent law firms have conducted comprehensive branding campaigns. And of those law firms that had conducted comprehensive branding campaigns, more than 55 percent planned to start one in the next twelve months.[1]

The bottom-line benefits of a strong professional service brand can be seen when you compare the hourly charge-out rates of the Big Four: PricewaterhouseCoopers, KPMG, Deloitte, and Ernst & Young, with their smaller, less well-known second tier competitors. For identical work the big firms consistently command significantly higher fees.

However, when it comes to professional service branding, few match the consultancy powerhouse McKinsey. Sometimes called the CEO's consultant, when McKinsey calls, CEOs open their doors.

How then do you successfully build a brand? How do you identify the often emotional variables that constitute a brand?

THE SIX DIMENSIONS OF BRAND IDENTITY | You'll never build a strong brand until you understand what the key elements are of a brand identity. Jean-Noel Kapferer in *Strategic Brand Management* [2] has come up with a highly practical model. Kapferer's brand model gives partners and managers in a professional service firm a common structure and language to discuss brand issues.

Kapferer's model also gives us a tool to assess the quality of brand management (Exhibit 9.1).

Kapferer's brand pyramid

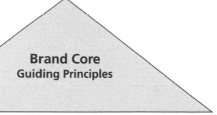

According to Kapferer the heart of the brand is the brand core. The brand core forms the brand essence. The brand core drives the brand and provides its very reason for existence. The core of the McKinsey brand is to provide independent, cutting-edge, research based, strategic advice.

The six dimensions

The identity of the brand is expressed through the six dimensions. The six dimensions are:

1. **Physical.** These are physical attributes or appearance—the name, colors, logo, and packaging.
2. **Reflection.** This is the image you reflect in your public communications, your brochures, advertising, and other public communications. Coca Cola typically shows young drinkers in its ads, even though its drinkers come from all age groups.
3. **Relationship.** This is how the brand portrays the way it relates to its customers. At Starbucks you can meet your friends and relax socially; Louis Vuitton offers access to an exclusive club.
4. **Personality.** This is the character of the brand. IBM's personality is seriously professional, while Apple's personality is creative and cool.
5. **Culture.** This refers to the background and values of the brand. Mercedes personifies German values of solidarity, reliability and excellence. Nike personifies "Just Do It."
6. **Self-Image.** This is how the customer sees herself in relation to the brand. When BodyShop buyers purchase cosmetics, they are also expressing support for a cleaner, greener environment.

BRAND STYLE

Culture, personality, and self-image form the brand style. Brand style should change only very slowly.

BRAND THEMES

Kapferer says the physical, relationship, and reflection dimensions form the brand themes. The themes may change as the brand evolves, or as new sub-brands develop.

HOW TO CLARIFY YOUR BRAND IDENTITY

Use the brand identity worksheet displayed in Exhibit 9.2 to clarify what your brand identity is—or could be. This will help you identify your six brand dimensions. Complete the brand identity worksheet by answering the following questions:

Dimension 1: Physical. What do our name, colors, logo, and packaging communicate to our clients about our image?

Dimension 2: Reflection. When we promote ourselves, what do we stand for in our advertisements, brochures, and presentations, what archetypal image of our target audience do we reflect? (For example, Coca Cola largely has young people in its ads, even though people of all ages drink Coke.)

Dimension 3: Relationship. How do we like to portray the way we relate to our clients? McKinsey, for example, portrays itself as the CEO's strategist. Louis Vuitton portrays itself as an exclusive club.

Dimension 4: Personality. What type of character do we like to project? For example, are we seriously professional like IBM, or are we young and creative like Apple?

Dimension 5: Culture. What values and heritage do we like to personify to our clients? Mercedes personifies German values of ruggedness and reliability.

Dimension 6: Self-Image. How do our clients see themselves when they do business with us? For example, BodyShop buyers see themselves as showing concern for the environment when they purchase.

THE POWER OF ARCHETYPES

Most professional firms struggle to find a unifying message that expresses what they stand for. In their book *The Hero and the Outlaw, Building Extraordinary Brands Through the Power of Archetypes,* Margaret Mark and Carol Pearson argue that today's most enduring and successful brands are built around ancient archetypes that leverage meaning.

"In ancient Greece and ancient Rome, archetypes formed the basis of myths, in which they were portrayed as gods and goddesses. In ancient Greece Nike was a winged goddess associated with victory.

EXHIBIT 9.2

**Brand identity
worksheet**

Brand Core
Guiding Principles

_____

_____

_____

Brand Themes	**Brand Style**
Physical: Appearance	**Culture:** Background and values
Reflection: Image of target audience	**Personality:** Brand character
Relationship: How the brand relates to the customer	**Self-Image:** How the customer relates to the brand

Nike the brand has simply lifted this archetypal imagery and turned it into one of the planets strongest brands."[3]

Mark and Pearson argue that archetypes are deeply embedded in our unconscious minds. Evoke an archetype in a customer's mind, they say, and you are able to tap into a set of powerful meanings that can be exploited.

Nike built its brand around what Mark and Pearson call the "Hero" archetype. The Hero archetype follows a simple but enthralling storyline. When everything seems lost, the hero rides over the hill and saves the day. In the 1990's Nike built its campaigns around sports hero Michael Jordan, who represented the ultimate in sporting "heroism." The marketing message was simple: super athletes wear Nikes.

The Sage Archetype

Mark and Pearson's research identified twelve archetypes. As far as branding for professional services goes, one archetype, the Sage, stands out.

According to Mark and Pearson, the Sage archetype is the expert who is always searching for truth. Brands that exploit the Sage archetype include Harvard University, MIT, McKinsey, and the Mayo Clinic. All of these organizations have built their brands around the discovery and dissemination of the truth.[4]

Isn't this what virtually all the best professional firms do?

Sage brands can disseminate information. Think of the *New York Times, Consumer Reports* and CNN.[5] Typically "they help the customer make smarter decisions." Isn't this what the best professional service firms do?

Sages are often called scholars, oracles, evaluators, advisers, philosophers, researchers, thinkers, planners, professionals, mentors, teachers, and contemplatives.[6] Aren't these the labels clients use to describe skilled professionals?

"Sage marketing is dignified and subdued with an elite air to exist," say Mark and Pearson. The most persuasive way to appeal to a Sage client, they feel, is to get an expert to endorse your brand.

THE SAGE TEST

According to Mark and Pearson, the Sage archetype can provide you with a suitable identity if:

- it provides expertise or information to your customer
- it encourages customers or clients to think
- the brand is based on a new scientific breakthrough or esoteric knowledge
- the quality of the brand is supported by hard data
- you are differentiating the product from others whose quality or performance is questionable.[7]

Most of our professional service clients fit these criteria perfectly. So, when you scrutinize your brand identity consider the Sage archetype.

LET ME TELL YOU A STORY | Marvin Bower helped found McKinsey & Co. Considered the father of modern management consulting, Bower wrote management bestsellers such as *The Will to Manage* (1966) and *The Will to Lead* (1997).

One important principle Bower taught was that consultants shouldn't be afraid to challenge a client's opinion.

McKinsey staff still recite the tale of when Bower bravely informed a major client that he, the head of the company, was the problem. Not surprisingly, McKinsey lost the client but that didn't bother Bower.

Firms such as McKinsey keep these stories alive because they communicate what makes their firms' value proposition distinctive.

Many professional firms have similar stories that have shaped their history and provide insights into the firms' values and approach to clients. These stories shouldn't just be left to become part of a firm's folklore. Stories such as these must be told and retold until they become part of the brand.

Stories work in four ways:
1. Stories grab a listener's attention. Like a movie, stories have a plot and characters for the audience to listen to.
2. Stories simplify complete ideas and make abstract concepts concrete.
3. Stories tap into the listener's emotions better than dry sets of facts.
4. Stories are memorable. A vivid story stays in a prospect's/client's mind long after everything else is forgotten.

The best stories "strike a deep nerve or reveal a deep truth"[8] that can be codified and embedded in all the firm's public communications.

Storytelling and PR

Robbie Vorhaus founded his own highly successful New York–based PR company Vorhaus Public Relations with the goal of helping recount their company's story using the structures of classic storytelling.

When it comes to illustrating classic storytelling in business, Robbie Vorhaus likes to offer the tale of Domino's Pizza.

> A young man who grows up in an orphanage goes into the Marines, returns and buys a small pizza store in Ypsilanti, Michigan, thinking he can make more money delivering pizza than waiting for customers to come to him. He opens

other stores, buys out his brother for the price of a VW, and builds the company into a $3.3 billion dollar global enterprise. He sells it for $1.1 billion and is quoted as saying, "I want to give all my money away and die broke." The theme here is: nothing takes the place of persistence.[9]

Vorhaus helps clients as diverse as Coca Cola, Buick, *PC Computing Magazine,* and the Boston University School of Law tell their stories. Vorhaus starts his storytelling work with clients by helping them uncover their core, unique selling proposition, or point of differentiation. Robbie Vorhaus's message is, "know your story, know your audience and tell your story better than anyone else."[10]

Many professional service firms have compelling stories that deserve to be told. This is not surprising when you think about the initial motivation that drives many students to become professionals in the first place. Students become doctors because they want to save lives. Students become lawyers because they want to right injustices. Students become architects because they want to design great buildings.

In many cases, successful professional firms have been built around the realization of these dreams. A great firm story can form the basis of a great brand.

DEVELOPING A BRAND PERSONA

A 125-year-old law firm, with eight offices spanning the southeastern United States, Womble, Carlyle, Sandridge & Rice has built up a solid reputation serving blue chip clients.

WINSTON, THE WOMBLE CARLYLE BULLDOG

In early 1996, the firm produced its first ad campaign. The ad that made by far the most emotional impact was one featuring a soulful bulldog.

Staff loved the bulldog. The bulldog resembled one of the most senior respected partners—"who is tenacious, loyal, sometimes pugnacious and above all fiercely protective of clients' interests."

The bulldog was so successful that the firm's marketing and design consultants created a firm bulldog named Winston (after the firm's founding officer).

Winston the bulldog became the centerpiece of a new ad campaign. Winston is now the centerpiece of vignettes that focus on such characteristics as "persistence, loyalty, dependability and vigilance—all very desirable characteristics of a champion bulldog or lawyer."

The bulldog imagery has been so successful that Winston has evolved into Womble Carlyle's brand. The bulldog also fits perfectly with the firm's tagline "Our lawyers mean business."[11]

The bulldog imagery captured the media's imagination. A feature article in a recent *bizlife* magazine was entitled "Bulldog of the Bar: Womble Carlyle Unleashes a New Breed of Lawyer Who Mean Business."[12]

Law firms find it difficult to differentiate themselves. So when clients tell Womble Carlyle staff that whenever they see a bulldog they think of Womble Carlyle, or conversely that when they hear or see the Womble Carlyle name they visualize the bulldog ads, they know they've succeeded. Womble Carlyle has created a powerful brand persona.[13]

APPOINT A BRAND COORDINATOR Creating and communicating a distinct personality for your practice takes time. Bottom-line rewards from a coherent brand program typically take three to five years to realize. We therefore suggest you set up a five-year fully budgeted brand development program and appoint a senior partner to oversee the program for all of that time.

Chopping and changing brand coordinators and branding programs is normally a recipe for disaster.

RESIST SHORT-TERM PRESSURES

It's extraordinarily tempting at times to sacrifice positioning and a brand's perceived value to engage in some pursuit that will help short-term sales and profits.

The most damaging short-term pressure comes from slashing prices in a downturn. If at all possible resist such pressures. The long-term damage can be irreparable. It is the task of the brand coordinator to lead the resistance to such moves.

Lessons from Athletic Shoes

Many professional firms think successful branding requires deep pockets combined with heavy advertising. When partners in small firms read about Accenture (formerly Andersen Consulting) spending $175 million on promoting its new name, they suck in their breath. So how do you take on the "big boys" and compete when you have limited funds? One of the best examples of how to outbrand a giant with deep pockets comes from the brutally competitive world of athletic footwear. Here, you might expect Nike to command the most brand loyalty—with Michael Jordan, Tiger Woods, and Mia Hamm on board as its celebrity endorsers.

But the highest levels of customer loyalty come from a company endorsed by no one, New Balance.

"New Balance has no celebrity endorsers, does minimal advertising, and yet in the last five years has gained more customer loyalty than any other athletic shoe brand," reports John Gaffney in *Business 2.0*.[14]

How? The fundamental reason is that New Balance offers a unique product: athletic shoes in varying widths. "No other athletic footwear manufacturer makes shoes for wide or narrow feet. . . . I can't tell you how many people tell me that we make the only shoes they can wear," says Paul Heffernan, New Balance vice president for global marketing.

Lesson for professional service firms: Successful branding starts with being able to offer unique, differentiated services.

New Balance targets serious athletes between 25 and 45. This group spends less than teens on sports shoes, but they are far more loyal.

Lesson for professional service firms: Identify and target the serious users of your services who will reward you with continued loyalty.

When New Balance does advertise and promote, it adopts a low-key approach. It advertises in niche magazines like *Outside, New England Runner,* and *Prevention* and the cable TV channels watched by older viewers.

Lesson for professional service firms: Focus your brand promotions around events your best clients attend. Adopt a soft-sell approach. If you do advertise, go for highly targeted niche publications.

Building Your Brand

Building a brand goes through three distinct phases.
Phase one: brand awareness. The first thing you have to do is to develop brand recognition. Prospects and clients need to know you exist.

Phase two: brand preference. You know you have reached the second phase when your target clients can articulate what sets you apart from your competitors.

Phase three: loyalty. When your target clients declare no one else can match them, or, I wouldn't consider anyone else, you have reached brand nirvana. This is how clients talk about the great brands of professional services.

TO ADVERTISE OR NOT TO ADVERTISE

When professionals buy into the importance of branding their first question is, "Where are we going to advertise?" Yet, in spite of the fact that the professional service firms are spending ever increasing amounts in advertising, there is little evidence to show that advertising is the best way to build a professional services brand.

Advertising has a massive credibility problem. According to the Pretesting Company, from 1986 to 1996 advertising believability plummeted from 61 percent to 38 percent. Disillusioned consumers simply don't believe the vast majority of advertising claims that "we're the best" or "we're number one."

Advertising agencies, which are also professional service firms, know this only too well. That's why they spend so little of their own marketing budget on advertising.

The evidence shows that public relations or ongoing publicity is much more effective and much cheaper than advertising, in building a professional service brand.

The same prospects who out of hand reject your firm's claims in an advertisement as self-serving and biased, take notice when an article in *Fortune* magazine quotes you as the leading authority in your field.

Public relations campaigns built around a core diet of articles, speeches, seminars, press releases, and occasional books are much more effective brand builders than advertisements. Why? Because these are the tools that establish your credentials.

So when does advertising work? According to Al Ries and Laura Ries, the authors of *The Fall of Advertising and the Rise of PR*, "the purpose of advertising is not to build a brand but to defend a brand, once the brand has been built by other means, primarily public relations or third party endorsements."[15]

Advertising That Works

After many years as a senior partner in a leading Vancouver family law firm, Lorne MacLean established his own firm to target a more upscale client base. His new firm, The MacLean Family Law Group used Ross Fishman Marketing and eLaw Marketing to create an appropriate brand and develop a multi-faceted marketing campaign. The key target audiences: referrals from local lawyers and affluent clients.

The multi-pronged marketing strategy included advertising, a tagline, brochures, e-mail marketing and a Web site. One highly visible tool was the four-ad print campaign, which used elegant black and white wedding photos of couples in love. The accompanying text is a series of heart-breaking, first-person narratives describing the decline of the relationship that led to the divorces. It shows the real, human, emotional side of the divorce practice. Instead of talking about the law firm, it puts the reader in the shoes of the couple, a powerful strategy.

In a second campaign, the firm featured an eye-catching image of a wedding cake. A bridge figurine stands alone on the top tier with tiny footsteps leading down the cake. In an instant the image conveys the anguish of divorce.

The copy for the four wedding invitation-style ads included:
> *"Our wedding was perfect.*
> *It was the marriage that sucked.*
> *At first, everything was great.*
> *The courtship, the ceremony, the honeymoon.*
> *But getting married and staying married are two different things*
> *And no one tells you about the reality of it.*
> *I got so wrapped up in the wedding that I never prepared for the marriage.*
> *In the end, I was not prepared for the day-to-day business of being a man and wife.*
> *Now, I am doing everything I can to prepare for this divorce."*

The ads finish with a brilliant tagline: *"We can't protect your heart. But we can protect your rights."* It then calls for the reader to take action: "Discuss your options with a divorce lawyer who has over twenty years of experience. MacLean Family Law Group 604 603 9000."

MacLean also used eLaw Marketing to create a HTML newsletter that linked to the firm's Web site.[16]

The campaign, conducted on a shoestring budget of under $20,000, grew profits by over 200 percent in the first year. The wedding cake ad generated lots of talk in the community and generated lots of direct referrals.

The campaign also won a 2003 Your Honor Award from the Legal Marketing Association.

ACTION
STEPS

1. Appoint a senior partner as brand coordinator.

2. Use the brand pyramid model to assess your current brand identity.

3. Use the brand pyramid model to define the brand personality you need to project to establish a competitive edge.

4. Consider using a Sage archetype to structure your firm's identity.

5. Recast your firm's history and achievements as a story.

6. Use the Womble Carlyle example to develop a brand persona. Ask, if your firm was an animal (or a car), what would it be?

7. Use the brand improvement program checklist to define the areas of priority and the steps you need to take to grow and strengthen your brand.

8. Commit your practice to the ongoing funding of a long-term (five years) brand development program.

CHAPTER 10

COUNTDOWN TO SUCCESS

How to transform your marketing plans into profits

Features •
• The five steps to success
• How to lead change

THE FIVE STEPS TO SUCCESS

"Make no little plans; they have no magic to stir men's blood and probably themselves will not be realized.   Make big plans; aim high in hope and work, remembering that a noble logical diagram once recorded will not die."

Daniel H. Burnham
American architect

Here is a five-step roadmap to help you implement an 8Rs integrated marketing program.

1. List and prioritize your practice's key marketing challenges.
2. Draw up a detailed marketing action plan (MAP).
3. Sell your vision and marketing action plan to all of your staff.
4. Compile a list of key performance metrics to measure the success of your marketing efforts.
5. Make all professional staff individually accountable for marketing and sales results.

STEP 1 : LIST AND PRIORITIZE YOUR KEY MARKETING CHALLENGES

Exhibit 10.1 provides a visual overview of the key actions you need to take to implement an integrated 8R-style marketing program. Use this exhibit and the more detailed action plans

EXHIBIT 10.1

The 8Rs growth and profitability formula

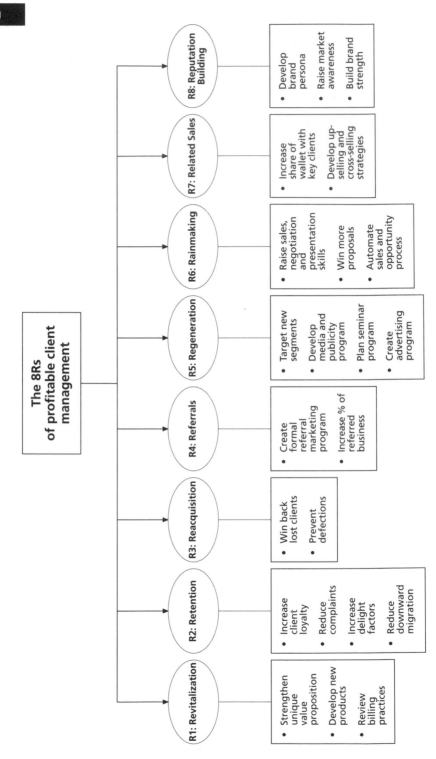

The 8Rs of profitable client management

R1: Revitalization
- Strengthen unique value proposition
- Develop new products
- Review billing practices

R2: Retention
- Increase client loyalty
- Reduce complaints
- Increase delight factors
- Reduce downward migration

R3: Reacquisition
- Win back lost clients
- Prevent defections

R4: Referrals
- Create formal referral marketing program
- Increase % of referred business

R5: Regeneration
- Target new segments
- Develop media and publicity program
- Plan seminar program
- Create advertising program

R6: Rainmaking
- Raise sales, negotiation and presentation skills
- Win more proposals
- Automate sales and opportunity process

R7: Related Sales
- Increase share of wallet with key clients
- Develop up-selling and cross-selling strategies

R8: Reputation Building
- Develop brand persona
- Raise market awareness
- Build brand strength

contained at the end of every chapter to prepare a list of your key marketing challenges. Prioritize your challenges by ranking them into a rough order of importance.

STEP 2 : DRAW UP A DETAILED MARKETING ACTION PLAN (MAP)

Exhibit 10.2 illustrates how to turn your list of priorities into a timetable plan built around 100-day blocks. To implement and lock-in a comprehensive marketing program, such as the one illustrated, would take most practices at least two years, so allow yourself adequate time.

STEP 3: SELL THE VISION AND MARKETING PLAN TO THE TEAM

A new approach to marketing can't be sold by e-mail or, for that matter, at a monthly partners' meeting. At the very least, all your senior staff need to be taken offsite for a two day retreat.

Start by presenting a compelling case for the need for change. Then paint a picture of what you could be if you are all prepared to launch a new marketing initiative.

Don't be too negative about your achievements so far. Stress that what you've done up to now has allowed you to become a *good firm*. What you want to do is to become a *great firm*. An 8R marketing program will help you do that.

Conclude the retreat with a plan for the future. Make sure you allow many opportunities for debate and participation. The most successful workshops usually include lots of mini-breakout sessions that allow time for members to discuss and argue over issues in small groups.

STEP 4: COMPILE A LIST OF KEY PERFORMANCE METRICS TO MEASURE THE SUCCESS OF THE PROGRAM

You can't manage what you can't measure. It is therefore critical that you draw up a list of measures that will allow you to track the success of your marketing.

EXHIBIT 10.2

Marketing action plan (MAP) based on the 8Rs—100 days campaign

	First 100 Days	2nd 100 Days	3rd 100 Days
Client Pyramid Management	• Set annual sales marketing goals based on pyramid analysis and market research • Prepare client contact campaigns for HVCs and potential HVCs*	• Allocate individual marketing plans to all professional staff • Prepare marketing metrics scorecard	
R1 Revitalization and Renewal	• Review competitive value proposition for each SBU** • Differentiate and position SBUs	• Identify profitable new segments/niches • Launch "new product" strategy	• Launch value pricing
R2 Retention		• Review client satisfaction measurement • Introduce "moments of truth" enhancement program	• Review complaints handling procedures • Begin service excellence training
R3 Reacquisition		• Initiate formal client win-back program	• Institute exit interviews for all defecting clients
R4 Referrals	• Introduce formal referral marketing campaign		
R5 Regeneration	• Develop publicity strategy • Plan small group seminar program • Develop email newsletter program • Plan advertising program	• Design model firm and SBU PowerPoint presentations	
R6 Rainmaking	• Psychologically test professional staff for rainmaking potential • Assess sales competencies	• Establish win-loss bid reporting system • Begin training in value added selling and negotiation skills	• Begin training in proposal writing • Review client contact and sales automation process
R7 Related Sales	• Develop up-selling and cross-selling strategy	• Identify additional profitable add-ons	• Train selected staff in up-selling and cross-selling
R8 Reputation Building	• Appoint brand coordinator	• Begin brand development program	

* high value clients
** strategic business unit

How many metrics should you track? Exhibit 10.3 lists thirty-one metrics. This list contains virtually all the marketing metrics professional service firms will ever need to measure.

However, different PSFs have different marketing priorities and therefore need different measures. Also, some PSFs don't bother to measure factors such as market size and market share because they find them so difficult to measure with any accuracy.

The base set of metrics contained in Exhibit 10.4 contains just fourteen measures. With this "top fourteen" you can track virtually all the key measures in an 8R marketing program.

Exhibit 10.4 also explains the significance of each metric. Most professional firms already compile the data that is needed for eleven of the listed metrics. Only three of the measures require client surveying or interviewing.

EXHIBIT 10.3		
Comprehensive list of marketing metrics	Size of target market ($)	Client retention (%)
	Target market growth (%)	Client satisfaction (%)
	Market share (%)	Client lifetime value ($)
	Sales ($)	Client delight (%)
	Profitability ($)	Clients who defected (no.)
	Profit per partner ($)	Lost clients regained (%)
	Revenue per professional ($)	Services sold to each client (no.)
	Utilization (%)	Share of client wallet (%)
	Profit as % of income (%)	Relative product/service quality (rank)
	Margin per client (%)	Relative new service sales (%)
	Average hourly rate ($)	Relative brand strength (rank)
	Sales growth (%)	Price premium (%)
	Successful sales closures (%)	New product launches (no.)
	New client acquisitions (no.)	Employee satisfaction (multipoint scale)
	Proposal bid to win ratio (%)	Professional staff turnover (%)
	Referral sourced sales (%)	

EXHIBIT 10.4

Base set of marketing metrics

Metric	Yardstick	Significance
1. Sales growth	Annual % change	Tracks revenue growth
2. Revenue per professional	$ value	Key indicator of staff productivity
3. Utilization	% of billable hours worked	Best measure of staff efficiency
4. Profit per partner	$ value	Prime financial success measure
5. Average hourly rate	$ rate	Measure of price premium
6. New client acquisitions	No. of new clients	Critical for growth
7. Referral sourced sales	% of new business	Cheapest and most valuable source of business
8. Client retention	% current clients	Key to long-term profitability
9. Client delight	Score on multipoint scale	Best indicator of client loyalty
10. Services sold to each client	No. of distinct services	Good cross-sell measure
11. Relative perceived quality	Rank compared to leading competitors	Good indicator of service quality
12. Brand recognition	% of target clients who recognize brand	Initial step in branding campaign
13. Staff satisfaction	Score on multipoint scale	Happy staff, key to client satisfaction
14. Professional staff turnover	% annual turnover	High turnover usually leads to quality and satisfaction issues

STEP 5 : MAKE ALL YOUR PROFESSIONALS INDIVIDUALLY ACCOUNTABLE FOR ACHIEVING MEASURABLE MARKETING AND SALES RESULTS

All professionals should be given their own marketing and sales plan which spells out specifically what they are expected to do, whether it be to win new business, present seminars, or write newsletters.

An equation for successful change

Installing a high performance marketing culture that generates high growth and super profits year after year requires leadership and sustained commitment.

Think of the 8Rs as a major change program. Columbia Business School uses a simple equation to show what is required for successful change to take place.

EXHIBIT 10.5

The equation for successful change

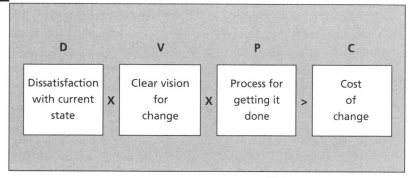

Source : Willie Pietersen, Reinventing Strategy, p. 191.[1]

D = Dissatisfaction. There needs to be *dissatisfaction* to induce change. Staff will refuse to change until they feel there is a real need. To sell the need for change, you need to answer the question "Why should we give up what we currently know and feel comfortable with?"

V = Vision. Successful change requires a path—a vision, a map. Where there is no vision, confusion and anxiety reign. So, sell and keep selling the vision and use your performance metrics to highlight your ongoing achievements.

P = Process. Successful change requires a step by step process. When it comes to marketing, busy professionals want to know what they need to do.

Note: the first three boxes in the equation must be multiplied by one another. So, if any of the boxes equals zero, the total of all three will add up to zero. This means that if any of the first three boxes (dissatisfaction, vision or process) are lacking, your change efforts will fail.

C = **Cost of Change.** The benefits of change must outweigh the costs and pains of change.

How to Lead Change: Six Golden Rules

Willie Pietersen, professor of management at Columbia University's Business School, says the leadership of change can be boiled down to six golden commonsense rules.

1. Create a simple, compelling statement of the case for change.
2. Communicate constantly and honestly.
3. Maximize participation.
4. If all else fails remove those who resist.
5. Generate short-term wins.
6. Set a shining example.[2]

Your odds of success will dramatically increase if you follow these rules when implementing the 8Rs.

Good luck!

APPENDIX 1

Exploiting the Internet

LEVERAGING E-COMMERCE

"The Internet is the world's least expensive and most efficient marketing tool and it helps companies of all sizes from all parts of the world disseminate sales and marketing messages, create one-to-one sales relationships, educate prospects and support existing customers on a worldwide scale," says author and online marketing expert Dan Janal.[1]

In spite of this fact few professional firms have come even close to maximizing the Internet's potential as a marketing tool. A few professional service firms have used the Web to transform their business. But for the vast majority of professional firms, the Internet remains little more than a place to park a brochure and digital business card.

THE INTERNET AND THE 8RS

Below is a list of suggestions of how you can integrate the Internet and our 8R marketing model.

R1: Revitalization

The Internet allows you to showcase and test new ideas, products, and services.

- Repackage intellectual property so it can be sold as downloadable digital products (software, PDFs).
- Conduct market research on possible new services and products with online surveys.

- Convert intangible services into products such as CD-ROMs, seminar kits, and audio tapes, which can be promoted and sold via the Web.
- Test and refine new service concepts with interactive PowerPoint demonstrations using a product such as OnlinePresenter. See www.presentationpro.com.

R2: Retention

One of the Internet's great advantages for professional service firms lies in its ability to strengthen and deepen existing client relationships and increase client loyalty.

- Fresh, compelling content in the form of articles, book reviews, and white papers will reinforce your expertise and trigger new needs.
- E-mail allows you to establish a one-to-one dialog with all of your clients, regardless of location.
- A members-only active area, which allows clients to access a range of exclusive services and products, allows you to show how much you value your existing clients.
- Set up a book review section where you review books relating to your area of expertise.
- Put an FAQ section on your site to answer lists of common queries.
- Educate clients and deepen customer loyalty by selectively e-mailing them selected articles on the latest developments in their industry that relate to your special area of expertise.
- Conduct customer satisfaction surveys by e-mail. With interactive feedback forms, clients can quickly tell you what they like and don't like.
- Use e-mail to survey your client's satisfaction after the completion of every job.
- Put all your newsletters online and create customizable sections for particular groups of clients.

R3: Reacquisition

Winning back lost clients can be a slow, tiresome, and frustrating process. The Web multiplies the opportunities for you to stay in regular contact with former clients whom you hope to win back.

- E-mail your former clients PowerPoint and PDF files of relevant presentations and seminars you've run, especially ones that showcase client success stories.
- Send newsletters to show off your services and demonstrate how you are continually improving the quality and value of your services.

R4: Referrals

The Internet is the ideal tool to leverage word-of-mouth marketing that forms the basis of successful networking.

- Use e-mail to distribute articles, handouts, and presentations inexpensively to your referral network.
- Participate in specialized newsgroups and online communities whose members have the potential to become referral sources.
- Generate referral revenue with links to affiliate merchant sites such as Amazon.com.
- Share resources and referrals with noncompeting online businesses that will in turn forward referrals back to you.

R5: Regeneration

The Internet allows you to dramatically lower the cost of attracting prospects.

- Focus on highly targeted, segmented groups of prospects with e-mail campaigns.
- Qualify prospects who visit your site by offering free white papers, software, or research in return for business or personal details.

- Educate customers with white paper articles, brochures, and other promotional tools.
- Deliver online PowerPoint presentations to targeted groups of clients through rich media, using e-mail tools such as EmailPresenter, at www.presentationpro.com.
- Use Web-conferencing and online meeting facilities such as WebEx (www.webex.com) to deliver online multimedia presentations, saving time and travel costs.
- Create lists of qualified prospects who initially come to your site searching for free content—e-zines, articles, white papers, or book reviews.
- Develop and maintain contacts with reporters by responding to questions quickly via e-mail and tailoring messages to each reporter's needs.
- Distribute press releases by e-mail to reporters promoting newsworthy events.

R6: Rainmaking

The Internet allows you to create and sell a new range of digitally driven services and products.

- Sell your services to new national and international markets.
- Visit competitors' Web sites to analyze how you compare and how to establish a competitive advantage.
- Sell downloadable digital online products such as reports, subscription newsletters and software.
- Use e-mail and your Web site to promote revenue earning events such as chargeable public seminars.
- Consider creating a lower-cost range of services that can only be accessed via the Web.
- Promote the services of associate organizations under your brand for which you receive a referral fee or commission.
- Form alliances with noncompeting companies that allow you to promote their services via your Web site.

R7: Related Sales

The Internet provides you with the opportunity to showcase and promote all of your service areas.

- Use your Web site and e-mail to promote your full range of services.
- Use the home page to promote different service areas by running special features or offers.
- Publish white papers on the pitfalls and risks of adopting adhoc approaches when buying services in your areas of expertise.
- When a client starts to purchase any base online product or service, offer a premium package as well and show them associated products that represent great value when bundled together.

R8: Reputation Building

A professional-looking Web site backed by compelling content allows you to brand yourself as a provider of premium services.

- Use the Web to promote your practice to a worldwide network of influential customers and associated professional groups.
- Establish yourself as a thought leader in your profession by publishing and distributing white papers, research articles, and books.
- Run Web-based PowerPoint slideshows to showcase your expertise.

THE 7Cs OF SUCCESSFUL E-COMMERCE

There is no simple magic formula for creating a compelling e-commerce Web site that attracts and makes clients want to purchase—again, again, and again.

The 7Cs—Content, Communication, Customer Care, Community, Convenience, Connectivity, and Customization—highlight the key ingredients of successful e-business.[2]

1. **Content**

   Compelling content forms the backbone of a successful professional service e-business. When prospects and clients visit your site, they look for access to the latest information and expert insights. These can take the form of free e-zines, white papers, articles, surveys, and book reviews.

   If you want the Web to be more than an access point for inquiries for your face-to-face services you have to create new, enticing Web-friendly products and services.

2. **Communication**

   The appearance of your site instantly communicates a certain look and feel. If your practice site looks good and oozes professional credibility, prospects will dig deeper.

   If your site design communicates poor design and cheapness, visitors will subconsciously devalue your practice.

   The copy you use to sell your services and products should be persuasive, benefit focused, and detailed enough to make the buyer make a quick, informed decision. Remember, the Web is still a word-based medium, so word choice and word use are critical.

   Pictures and graphics create visual appeal. However, beware large graphics which are a turn-off because of slow download times.

   Above all, clients also want dialog (e-mail, live chat, online surveys) and interactivity.

3. **Customer Care**

   Successful customer care is based on receiving optimal levels of support at all stages of the relationship.

   Clients look for e-mail, toll-free numbers, and FAQ pages, and expect to get their questions answered when they need them to be.

   Clients look for immediate recognition when they place orders and expect ongoing status reports on the resolution of orders.

Since clients don't want to be dictated to, they prefer a choice of payment, delivery, and return options.

Behind all the technology they look for knowledgeable, well-trained staff empowered to resolve complaints.

Finally, customer care is underpinned by transparent security and privacy policies that aggressively protect client confidentiality.

4. **Community**

"The best sites provide users with expert information in a clear and entertaining style, and give them a chance to react and interact with other businesses," says A. T. Kearney.[3]

Chatrooms and discussion boards deepen relationships and reinforce client loyalty.

5. **Convenience**

Usability is critical. If a client can't find a product or service, then he or she will not purchase it.

Whenever you scan a Web page, everything should be "self-evident, obvious, self-explanatory," says usability author Steve King.[4] Anything that makes us stop, ponder, and puzzle erodes our confidence. A site must be easy to use, easy to navigate, intuitively organized, and built for quick transactions.

Clients won't tolerate problem-ridden, unstable sites. Your site has to load quickly, graphics must download in an instant, and search functions have to be intuitive and accurate.

6. **Connectivity**

Web users like clicking onto links to other sites that offer relevant complementary information, products, and services.

For links to add value, they have to be easy to find, up-to-date, and arranged logically.

Links to affiliates can provide significant extra revenue as well as attract further enquiries.

7. **Customization**

Site stickiness and sales increase significantly when you can customize and personalize what you offer to each buyer.

You can customize buyers' experiences by allowing them to choose the information they wish to view.

The Web's ability to track a customer's pages visited and purchase history means you can tailor products and services to meet individual clients and targeted groups' needs.

Buyers therefore expect online businesses to know their purchase history and tailor their services to match.

Treat the 7Cs as a set of guidelines rather than a set formula. "Some companies will need all the 7Cs, while others may only need five. Ultimately, the Cs used will depend on the company and its stage of the customer relationship," according to Kearney.[5]

Professional service firm e-commerce performance survey

Use this survey to assess your e-commerce efforts.

The importance of each item varies from business to business and depends upon your stage of commerce development.

E=Excellent	5=Extremely important
VG=Very Good	4=Important
G=Good	3=Somewhat important
F=Fair	2=Neutral
P=Poor	1=Not at all important

	Performance	Importance	Comments
Content			
• Up-to-date, relevant, insightful content geared toward target customers	E VG G F P	1 2 3 4 5	
• Differentiated, enticing products or services	E VG G F P	1 2 3 4 5	
• Pictures with mini CVs of key personnel	E VG G F P	1 2 3 4 5	
• Testimonials from respected clients	E VG G F P	1 2 3 4 5	
Communication			
• Purpose of site and intended audience clear	E VG G F P	1 2 3 4 5	
• Attractive, distinctive, professional looking site	E VG G F P	1 2 3 4 5	
• Home page outlines purpose and description of site	E VG G F P	1 2 3 4 5	
• Home page shows visitors how to locate whatever you want to find	E VG G F P	1 2 3 4 5	
• Enticing home page overviews of what site has to offer	E VG G F P	1 2 3 4 5	
• Home page promotes key features, promotions	E VG G F P	1 2 3 4 5	

• Multiple opportunities for two-way interaction and dialog
  - e-mail
  - live chat
  - online surveys
  - discussion forums
	E VG G F P	1 2 3 4 5	

Customer care			
• Verifiable e-commerce security	E VG G F P	1 2 3 4 5	
• Guaranteed personal privacy	E VG G F P	1 2 3 4 5	
• Choice of payment, delivery, and return options	E VG G F P	1 2 3 4 5	
• Responsive query and complaint handling process	E VG G F P	1 2 3 4 5	
• FAQ pages	E VG G F P	1 2 3 4 5	

• Knowledgeable, well-trained support staff	E VG G F P	1 2 3 4 5	
• Track status and location of order	E VG G F P	1 2 3 4 5	
• Toll-free support number	E VG G F P	1 2 3 4 5	
Community			
• Discussion forum for target clients	E VG G F P	1 2 3 4 5	
• Links to related specialist sites	E VG G F P	1 2 3 4 5	
Convenience			
• User-friendly site architecture	E VG G F P	1 2 3 4 5	
• Intuitive, user-friendly navigation	E VG G F P	1 2 3 4 5	
• Clear, concise, error-free writing	E VG G F P	1 2 3 4 5	
• Inviting and informative home page	E VG G F P	1 2 3 4 5	
• Easy to initiate and complete commercial transaction	E VG G F P	1 2 3 4 5	
• Fast download times for all pages, graphics, and documents	E VG G F P	1 2 3 4 5	
• Intuitive, accurate search function	E VG G F P	1 2 3 4 5	
• Easy to skim and scan Web pages	E VG G F P	1 2 3 4 5	
• Clear visual hierarchy on each page	E VG G F P	1 2 3 4 5	
• Pages broken into clearly defined areas	E VG G F P	1 2 3 4 5	
• Navigation system shows you where you are, where you have been, and where you can go	E VG G F P	1 2 3 4 5	
• Navigation shortcuts that allow you to move through the site quickly and efficiently	E VG G F P	1 2 3 4 5	
Connectivity			
• Links to other industry related Web sites relevant to visitor's interests	E VG G F P	1 2 3 4 5	
• Links to commercial affiliate sites	E VG G F P	1 2 3 4 5	
• All links to other sites open with windows that make the visitor return to your site before exiting	E VG G F P	1 2 3 4 5	
Customization			
• Surfer can customize experience by choosing what type of information they view	E VG G F P	1 2 3 4 5	
• Client-offered tailored service or product offer based on past purchase history	E VG G F P	1 2 3 4 5	

N O T E S

Chapter 1

1 Wendy M. Becker, Miriam F. Herman, Peter A. Samuelson, and Allen P. Webb, "Lawyers Get Down to Business," *McKinsey Quarterly,* 2001, Number 2, p. 45.

2 Jim Schroeder, "The Am Law 200: The Second Hundred's Hidden Strength," *The American Lawyer,* August 1, 2002.

3 Idea adapted from Scott Davis, *Brand Asset Management,* Jossey-Bass, 2000, pp. 208-212.

4 Peter Doyle, *Value Based Marketing,* Wiley, 2000, pp. 80-81.

5 Chris Fritsch, reported in "Initiating an Effective Client Survey Program," Lawmarketing.com, December 18, 2001.

6 Anthony J. Zahorik, Roland T. Rust, Timothy L. Keiningham, "Estimating the Return on Quality," *Handbook of Services Marketing,* ed. Teresa A. Swartz and Dawn Iacobucci, Sage, 2000, p. 235.

7 Quoted in Chris Fritsch, "Initiating an Effective Client Survey Program," Lawmarketing.com, December 18, 2001.

8 Lisa Endlich, *Goldman Sachs, The Culture of Success,* Warner, 1999, p. 238.

9 Jeffrey J. Fox, *How to Become a Rainmaker,* Hyperion, 2000, p. 18.

10 Ibid.

11 Harry Beckwith, *The Invisible Touch,* Warner Books, 1997, pp. 98-99.

Chapter 2

1 Thomas J. Kosnik, *How to Assess and Build A Company's Reputation.* Case no. 589-087. Beston: Harvard Business School, 1989. Copyright © 1989 by the Presidents and Fellows of Harvard Business College. Reprinted by permission.

2 www.WLRK.com

3 Charles J. Fombrun, *Reputation,* Harvard Business School Press, 1996, pp. 26-27.

4 B. Joseph Pine II, James H. Gilmore, *The Experience Economy,* HBS, 1999, p. 21.

5 Bernd H. Schmitt, *Experiential Marketing,* The Free Press, p.22.

6 Colin Shaw and John Ivens, *Building Great Customer Experiences,* Palgrave, 2002, p. 10.

7 Robert G. Cooper and Scott J. Edgett, *Product Development for the Service Sector,* Perseus Books, 1999, p. 9.

8 Ibid., p. 29.

9 Ibid., p. 11.

10 "A Rose by Any Name," *Forbes Global,* March 4, 2002, p. 61.

Chapter 3

1 Werner Reinartz and V. Kumar, "The Mismanagement of Customer Loyalty," *Harvard Business Review,* July 1, 2002, pp. 86-94.

2 Tony Cram, *The Power of Relationship Marketing,* Pitman, 1994, p. 107.

3 See Burke white paper series, www.burke.com

4 Jan Carlzon, *Moments of Truth,* Ballinger, 1987, p. 23.

5 Jill Griffin, *Customer Loyalty,* Jossey-Bass, 1995, p. 135.

6 Richard B. Chase and Sriram Dasu, "Want to Perfect Your Company's Service?," *Harvard Business Review,* June 2001, pp. 79-84.

7 Ibid., p. 82.

8 Ibid., p. 83.

9 Ibid., p. 84.

10 Ibid.

11 Stephanie Coyles and Timothy C. Gokey, "Customer Retention Is Not Enough," *McKinsey Quarterly,* 2002, Number 2, www.mckinseyquarterly.com

12 Ibid.

13 Ibid.

Chapter 4

1 Jill Griffin and Michael W. Lowenstein, *Customer Win-Back,* Jossey-Bass, © 2001, pp. 5–10. This material is used by permission of John Wiley & Sons, Inc.

2 Ibid., pp. 8–9.

3 Ibid., p. 9.

4 Ibid.

5 B. Strauss and C. Friege, "Regaining Service Customers," *Journal of Service Research,* May 1999, p. 351.

6 Jill Griffin, Ibid., pp. 109–117. Used by permission of John Wiley & Sons, Inc.

7 Ibid., pp. 72–85. Used by permission of John Wiley & Sons, Inc.

8 Ibid., p. 66. Used by permission of John Wiley & Sons, Inc.

Chapter 5

1 Ford Harding, *Creating Rainmakers,* Adams, 1998, p. 20.

2 Ivan R. Misner, *The World's Best Known Marketing Secret,* Bard, 1994, pp. 69-90.

3 Elisabeth L. Misner, "The Wise Farmer," *Masters of Networking,* ed. Ivan R. Misner, and Don Morgan, Bard, 2000, p. 262.

4 Ivan R. Misner PhD & Robert Davis, *Business by Referral,* Bard Press, 1998, pp. 48-50.

5 Bob Burg, *Endless Referrals,* McGraw-Hill, 1998.

6 John Warrillow, *Drilling for Gold,* John Wiley, 2002, pp. 92–93. This material is used by permission of John Wiley & Sons, Inc.

7 "McKinsey's Influence at the Top Table," *Sunday Business Times,* October 1, 2000.

8 "CEO Superbowl," *Fortune,* August 2, 1999.

9 Conversations with former McKinsey staff.

10 Cem Sertoglu and Anne Berkowitch, "Cultivating Ex Employees," *Harvard Business Review,* June 2002, p. 21.

11 Ibid.

Chapter 6

1 David Siegel, www.KillerSites.com

2 Philip Kotler, Thomas Hayes, Paul N. Bloom, *Marketing Professional Services,* Prentice Hall, 2002, p. 176.

3 Craig Terrill and Arthur Middlebrooks, *Market Leadership Strategies for Service Companies,* NTC, 1999, pp. 56-63.

4 Ibid.

5 Philip Kotler, *Kotler on Marketing,* Free Press, 1999, p. 27.

6 Ibid.

7 Ibid.

8 Herman Simon, *Hidden Champions,* Harvard Business School Press, 1996.

9 www.rossfishmanmarketing.com/crosslin_slaten_o'connor

10 Kevin Brown, kb@kevinbrownmarketing.com

11 Reece Franklin, *The Consultant's Guide to Publicity,* John Wiley, 1996, p. 64.

12 David R. Yale with Andrew J. Carothers, *The Publicity Handbook,* McGraw-Hill, 2001, pp. 13-14.

13 David E. Gumpert, *Do-It-Yourself Public Relations: A Success Guide for Lawyers,* ABA, 1995, pp. 61–66.

14 Larry Bodine, "How to Make Friends with Reporters and Influence the Press," November 1999. Larry Bodine is a Web and Marketing Consultant based in Glen Ellyn, IL, lbodine@lawmarketing.com

15 Robert W. Bly, *The Six Figure Consultant,* Upstart, 1998, pp. 27-28.

16 David E. Gumpert, Ibid., p. 74.

17 Robert W. Bly, Ibid., pp. 27-28.

18 Bruce Marcus, *Competing for Clients in the 1990's,* McGraw-Hill, 1992, p. 91.

19 "The Find 'Em and Keep 'Em Toolkit," *New Zealand Post,* 1997, pp. 122-123.

20 Richard S. Hodgson, *The Greatest Direct Mail Sales Letters of All Time,* Dartnell, 1995, p. 13.

21 Bob Stone, *Successful Direct Marketing Methods,* 5th ed., NTC, 1994, pp. 385-386.

22 Robert W. Bly, Ibid., Appendix F: Sample Documents.

23 www.jupiterresearch.com

24 Seth Godin, *Permission Marketing,* Simon & Schuster, 1999.

25 Adapted from "The Basics of Campaign Development," www.boldfish.com

26 David M. Freedman, "12 Seminal Tips for Promotional Newsletters," 2000, nswltr.com

27 Mark Pruner, "Newsletter Marketing," www.findlaw.com, October 30, 2001.

28 Rachel McAlpine, *Web Word Wizardry,* Corporate Communications, 1999, p. 87.

29 Mark Pruner, Ibid.

30 Ibid.

31 "Law Firm Marketing Budgets," www.legalmarketing.org, Harris Interactive, 2001.

32 Philip Kotler, Thomas Hayes, and Paul N. Bloom, *Marketing Professional Services,* Prentice Hall, 2002, p. 335.

33 Ibid.

34 Anthony O. Putman, *Marketing Your Services,* John Wiley, 1990, p. 188.

35 Ibid.

36 Sarah White, *The Complete Idiot's Guide to Marketing Basics,* Macmillan, p. 251.

37 Anthony O. Putnam, Ibid., p. 277.

38 Sarah White, Ibid., pp. 234-235.

Chapter 7

1 Herb Greenberg, Harold Weinstein, and Patrick Sweeney, *How to Hire and Develop Your Next Top Performer,* McGraw-Hill, 2001.

2 Ibid., p. 30.
3 Ibid.
4 Ibid., p. 61.
5 Ibid., pp. 155–156.
6 Peter Bartram, "Winning new business, the two worlds of accountancy," www.accountingweb.co.uk, June 26, 2001.
7 Ibid.

Chapter 8

1 Jay Abraham, *Getting Everything You Can Out of All You've Got,* St. Martin's Press, 2000, pp. 123-124.

Chapter 9

1 *Law Firm Marketing Budgets,* Legal Marketing Association, 2001, p. 4.
2 Jean-Noel Kapferer, *Strategic Brand Management,* Kogan Page, 1997, pp. 90–119.
3 Margaret Mark and Carol S. Pearson, *The Hero and the Outlaw,* McGraw-Hill, 2001, p. 5.
4 Ibid., p. 89.
5 Ibid., p. 90.
6 Ibid.
7 Ibid., p. 100.
8 Ibid., p. 291.
9 Robbie Vorhaus, www.storytelling.com/news/abt_RV_interview

10 Ibid.
11 Paula G. Blanchat, *www.wcsr.com,* Pressroom for Womble Carlyle Sandridge & Rice, PLLC.
12 "Bulldog of the Bar," *bizlife* magazine, June 2001.
13 Paula G. Blanchat, *www.wcsr.com,* Pressroom for Womble Carlyle Sandridge & Rice, PLLC.
14 John Gaffney, "Shoe Fetish," *Business 2.0,* March 2002.
15 Al Ries and Laura Ries, *The Fall of Advertising and the Rise of PR,* Harper Business, 2002, p. xiv.
16 www.rossfishmanmarketing.com

Chapter 10

1 Willie Pietersen, *Reinventing Strategy,* John Wiley, 2002, p. 191.
2 Ibid., pp. 195-196.

Appendix 1

1 Daniel S. Janal, *Dan Janal's Guide to Marketing on the Internet,* John Wiley, 2000, p. 36.
2 A.T. Kearney, "E-Business Performance," White paper, www.atkearney.com
3 Ibid.
4 Steve King, *Don't Make Me Think,* Que, 2000, p. 11.
5. A.T. Kearney, Ibid.

INDEX

Apple, 236, 237
archetypes in branding, 237, 239–240
Arthur Andersen, 18, 67
at-risk clients *see also* reacquisition;
retention
    defection of, 12–14
    detection of, 99
    strategy for saving, 101–103
AT&T, 38
availability only retainers, 70
awards, value of winning, 51–52

B

Baker Scholars, 38
BATNA (Best Alternative to a
Negotiated Agreement), 207
benefits focus strategy, 125–126
Benesch Friedlander Coplan and
Aronoff LLP, 165
Betty Crocker, 54
"Big Four" accounting firms
    branding, 234
    delivery of web-based services, 6
    impact of deregulation on, 5
billboard advertising, 176
billing *see* pricing
Bly, Bob, 147, 149
Bodyshop, 236, 237
book publishing, power of, 48–49 *see
also* publication
Booz Allen, 39
Boston Consulting Group (BCG),
42–44
Boston matrix, 43–44
Bower, Marvin, 37–39, 240
brand coordinator, appointment of,
243–244
brand identity
    brand personas, 242–243
    clarification of, 236–237
    Kapferer's key elements, 234–236
    power of archetypes, 237, 239–240
    storytelling, 240–242
    worksheet, 238

brand pricing, 9
branding
    advertising and, 246–248
    benefits of, 20–21, 234
    effectiveness of, 233
    New Balance example, 244–245
    phases of brand building, 245
broadcast advertising, 176
bronze clients, 15, 17
Buick, 242
business publications, advertising in,
175

C

"cash cow diagram", 43–44
Chambers of Commerce, 117
Champy, James, 45, 46
change management, 257–258
channel access focus strategy, 126
Chuck E. Cheese, 54
client base, regeneration of *see*
regeneration
client defection *see* defection
client evaluation profile, 81
client expectations, management of,
88–89
client loyalty *see* loyalty
client newsletters
    benefits of, 165
    e-mail newsletters
        benefits of, 167–168
        expansion of mailing list, 172
        failure to follow through, 171
        feedback, 171
        formats, 168
        techniques for writing, 169–170
        tracking results, 170–171
    promotion of, 166–167
    types, 165–166
client pyramid analysis
    analysis of migration patterns, 30–31
    inerts, 28
    live leads, 28
    process of, 25–28

e-commerce performance survey,
269–270
rainmaking, 264
reacquisition, 263
referrals, 263
regeneration, 263–264
related sales, 265
reputation building, 265
retention, 262
revitalization, 261–262
iron clients, 15, 17

J

joint ventures, 71
Jordan, Michael, 239, 244

K

Kapferer's brand model, 234–236
Kellogg School of Management, 37, 51
Korn Ferry, 5
KPMG, 172, 234

L

lead generation
   direct mail, use of, 157
   referrals see referrals
leadership
   change management, 258
   market leadership see market
   leadership
letter writing see direct mail
Levins, Alan, 49
LexisNexis, 6
licensing, 71
lines of business focus strategy,
124–125
Linklaters & Alliance, 5
Littler Mendelson, 49, 222
live leads
   definition of, 28
   goal setting for, 29
local market focus strategy, 126
loss making clients, 17–18

lost clients see reacquisition
Louis Vuitton, 236, 237
loyalty see also retention
   buyers of multiple services, 221
   classification of clients, 80, 83
   complaint handling and, 87–88
   creation of ``wow" experiences, 86
   downward migration, 91–92
   economics of, 77–78
   first-time clients, treatment of, 89
   indicators of long-term loyalty, 82
   over-dependence on key clients,
   10–11
   referrals and, 107
   satisfaction/loyalty link, 83–86

M

McDonalds, 54
McKinsey & Co, 5, 36, 37–39, 42, 45,
47, 48, 118, 234, 235, 237, 239, 240–241
MacLean Family Law Group, 247–248
magazines, advertising in, 175
management of client expectations,
88–89
market leadership
   differentiation of services by, 35–39
   leadership positionings, 37
market segmentation
   niche marketing, 136–137
   process of, 128–135
   purpose of targeting segments, 128
   supplier of first choice, 128
   targeting single segments, 136
market specialization, 39–42, 124, 125
Marketing Deficiency Syndrome
(MDS)
   branding, 20–21
   client loyalty, 10–11
   client relationship strategy
      differentiation by needs, 15–16
      purpose of, 14
      segmentation by value, 14–15
      upgrading clients, 16–17
   defection of clients, 12–14
   effect of, 6

S

Sales IQ test, 186–191
sales process
  closing the sale, 203–206
  competitive analysis, 202–203
  credibility, 193–196
  identification of decision makers, 195–196
  negotiation
    BATNA, 207
    buyer types, 206
    purpose of, 206
    relationship buyers, 210–211
    transaction buyers, 207–210
  objections, handling of, 204–205
  OPEN questioning process, 197–200
  performance analysis, 218
  proposing solutions, 200–203
  sales presentations, 213–215
  sales proposals, 212–213
  setting call objectives, 194
  SOFTEN approach, 194
  sponsors, use of, 196
  uncovering and developing needs, 196–200
  win-loss reports, 215–217
sales targets, setting of, 29–30
salespeople *see* rainmaking
Salomon Brothers, 61
satisfaction surveys *see* client satisfaction surveys
Scandinavian Airlines, 86
Schlossberg, David, 20–21
segmentation *see* market segmentation
seminars
  charging for, 140
  guidelines, 139–141
  ideal topics, 139
  purpose, 138
  types, 138–139
services *see* professional services
silver clients, 15, 16, 17
Siskind, Greg, 126
Skadden, Ross, Slate, Meagher and
Flom, 51–52
SOFTEN approach, 194
specialization, 39–42, 124, 125
sponsors, use of, 196
Starbucks, 54, 55, 236
Stern Stewart & Co, 46
stock options, 71
storytelling, use of, 240–242
streamlined services, 125
success fees, 71
supplier of first choice, 128
SWOT analysis, 56, 59

T

technological change, effect of, 6
television advertising, 176
tender, 70
tests
  rainmaking, 180
  reacquisition, 94
  referrals, 106
  regeneration, 120
  related sales, 220
  reputation building, 232
  retention, 76
  revitalization, 34
The Global Institute, 39
The Monitor Group, 48
Three Es Model of buying professional services, 191–193
time-based charging, 70
TMP Worldwide, 6
toxic clients, 18
trade associations, networking and, 117
Treacy, Michael, 48
Tuck School of Business, 51

U

undifferentiated services, 7–8, 35
Ungaretti & Harris, 52, 53
unique selling proposition (USP), 55
unique value proposition (UVP)
  checklist of differentiators, 57–58

nature of, 55–56
up-selling *see* cross-selling and up-selling

V

value pricing, 9, 67–74
visalaw.com, 126
visual aids, use of, 143–145
Vorhaus, Robbie, 241–242

W

Wachtell, Lipton, Rosen & Katz, 40–41, 61
Waterman, Robert, 47
Web marketing *see* Internet marketing
wedge projects, 224–225
Westlaw, 6
Wharton School, 36–37
Wiersema, Fred, 48

win-back policies *see* reacquisition
win-loss reports, 215–217
winning awards, value of, 51–52
Womble, Carlyle, Sandridge & Rice, 242–243
Woods, Tiger, 244
"wow" experiences, 86
writing articles *see* publication
writing letters *see* direct mail

X

Xerox, 84

Y

Yellow Pages, advertising in, 174
Young Entrepreneurs Organization (YEO), 117
Young Presidents Association (YPA), 117

ABOUT THE AUTHOR

The chief executive of The Mills Group, an international consulting and training firm, Harry Mills has spent seventeen years consulting and training over 3,000 partners and managers in accounting, legal, consulting, and professional service firms all over the globe.

Harry Mills' professional service clients include three of the Big Four giants: PricewaterhouseCoopers, KPMG, and Ernst & Young. At the same time, Harry Mills has worked with dozens of mid-sized and small legal, consulting, engineering, and other professional service firms.

The Mills Group's corporate clients include IBM, Ericsson, Oracle, BMW, Toyota, Lexus, and Unilever. Many of the insights in the Mills Group professional service practice have come from lessons learned while working with these world-renowned marketers.

Harry Mills is the best-selling author of twenty-two books on sales, persuasion and negotiation, including *Clinch That Deal, Sales Secrets* and *The Mental Edge*. The American Chamber of Commerce called Harry's latest book, *Artful Persuasion: How to Command Attention, Change Minds and Influence People,* "one of the best books ever written on persuasion."

Harry is also a subject matter expert and mentor for the Harvard Business School's ManageMentor program on persuasion.

A regular keynote speaker at international conferences, Harry also appears regularly on television and radio to comment on business issues. He has been featured in *Entrepreneur* magazine, *BottomLine Business, Sales & Marketing Management* and *USA Today*.

Harry Mills can be contacted at harry.mills@millsonline.com. The Mills Group Web site, www.millsonline.com, offers further tools and a complete range of supporting services.